I0416443

August 2012

IRAQ AND AFGHANISTAN

State and DOD Should Ensure Interagency Acquisitions Are Effectively Managed and Comply with Fiscal Law

GAO
Accountability ★ Integrity ★ Reliability

GAO-12-750

August 2012

IRAQ AND AFGHANISTAN

State and DOD Should Ensure Interagency Acquisitions Are Effectively Managed and Comply with Fiscal Law

Highlights of GAO-12-750, a report to congressional committees

Why GAO Did This Study

State has taken on unprecedented responsibilities in Iraq and Afghanistan. In doing so, it has relied heavily on contractors. For some critical goods and services, such as fuel, security, and basic support like dining and laundry services, State turned to DOD to acquire the goods and services on its behalf through interagency acquisitions. Because of the risks associated with assisted interagency acquisitions, agencies need to carefully consider whether their use is a sound business decision and formally document roles and responsibilities in interagency agreements.

To better understand how State is managing its responsibilities in Iraq and Afghanistan, GAO evaluated (1) the nature and extent of State's reliance on DOD for the acquisition of critical goods and services, (2) factors that contributed to this reliance, and (3) whether State and DOD are making and implementing decisions regarding this reliance consistent with regulation and guidance. GAO reviewed documentation for 22 acquisitions, including State's requests for assistance, comparing them to regulation and guidance.

What GAO Recommends

GAO recommends that State assess its planning for sufficient and appropriate acquisition personnel and that State and DOD take certain steps to bring existing and planned interagency acquisitions into compliance with regulation and guidance and resolve their positions on State's payment for DOD's services. Both State and DOD agreed with the recommendations.

View GAO-12-750. For more information, contact John P. Hutton at (202) 512-4841 or huttonj@gao.gov.

What GAO Found

To help the Department of State (State) meet its requirements for critical goods and services in Iraq and Afghanistan, the Department of Defense (DOD) supported State on 22 acquisitions. On State's behalf, DOD awarded and manages 20 acquisitions, known as assisted interagency acquisitions, under the authority of the Economy Act with an estimated value of almost $1 billion for basic support goods and services and security services. DOD also supported two of State's acquisitions for medical services and unmanned aerial vehicles. Across the 22 acquisitions, DOD has been involved in one or more aspects of the acquisition cycle, including planning, award, management, and oversight. GAO identified at least 128 DOD personnel with contracting and subject matter expertise who provided support for these acquisitions.

In justifying requests in 2010 for DOD's acquisition assistance, State officials cited the urgency of ensuring requirements were met as the two departments prepared for U.S. military forces to withdraw from Iraq at the end of 2011. Underlying that sense of urgency was the insufficient capacity and expertise of State's acquisition workforce. Specifically, State and DOD concluded that State lacked sufficient personnel, both in numbers and expertise, to conduct acquisition activities and that it did not have the requisite time to increase its workforce to the capacity required to have contracts in place following the transition to a State-led presence in Iraq. State has taken some steps to address the acquisition workforce gaps that prompted it to seek DOD's help. However, State has not fully assessed whether its effort to increase its workforce is sufficient to meet requirements; it has the proper skill and government/contractor mix; or it has sufficient numbers of qualified oversight personnel to support its own acquisition efforts in Iraq and Afghanistan in the future.

State and DOD did not comply with requirements for use and management of assisted acquisitions. For 12 of the 20 assisted acquisitions GAO reviewed, State did not comply with Office of Management and Budget and Federal Acquisition Regulation requirements for determining that using DOD contracts was the best procurement approach. For example, State did not assess the cost-effectiveness of using DOD's contracts for five of the interagency acquisitions. Further, State and DOD did not meet requirements for interagency acquisition agreements in 13 cases, resulting in confusion regarding oversight responsibilities and payment for DOD's assistance. Accordingly, the departments' positions regarding State's payment of DOD's costs prior to 2012 in connection with the award and administration of some acquisitions remain unresolved and the departments risk noncompliance with fiscal law. Some lessons have been learned since State's 2010 requests for DOD's acquisition assistance in Iraq. However, poor compliance with interagency acquisition requirements and missed opportunities to fully understand costs and needs for goods and services continue to limit State's ability to conduct acquisition planning. Over the next 18 months, as key contracts for Iraq are set to expire and the U.S. presence in Afghanistan evolves, the departments' opportunity is shrinking to determine whether continued reliance is appropriate or State should develop its own capacity. Otherwise, State risks again relying on assisted acquisitions with DOD by default rather than through sound business decisions.

_____ United States Government Accountability Office

Contents

Figures

Abbreviations

AQM	Office of Acquisitions Management
CENTCOM	U.S. Central Command
COR	contracting officer's representative
DCAA	Defense Contract Audit Agency
DCMA	Defense Contract Management Agency
DLA	Defense Logistics Agency
DOD	Department of Defense
FAR	Federal Acquisition Regulation
FIRST	Field and Installation Readiness Support Team
LOGCAP	Logistics Civil Augmentation Program
OMB	Office of Management and Budget
OPE	Office of the Procurement Executive
SSS-I	Security Support Services-Iraq
TWISS	Theater Wide Internal Security Services
UAV	Unmanned Aerial Vehicle

United States Government Accountability Office
Washington, DC 20548

August 2, 2012

Congressional Committees

The Department of State (State) has taken on unprecedented responsibilities in support of U.S. government efforts in Iraq and Afghanistan. In December 2011, when the last U.S. military brigade left Iraq pursuant to the Security Agreement between the United States and the Government of Iraq, State and the Department of Defense (DOD) completed the largest military-to-civilian transition since the Marshall Plan at the end of World War II. In assuming responsibility from DOD for leading the U.S. presence, State has primary responsibility for not only carrying out its diplomatic mission but also providing critical goods and services to support all U.S. government personnel in Iraq, as well as some contractor personnel. These critical goods and services include security, medical, and basic support such as food, fuel, dining, laundry, and waste management. In Afghanistan, as DOD plans for a reduction in U.S. military forces, State plans to draw on its experiences in Iraq to prepare for similarly expanded responsibilities. In the future, such responsibilities may not be unique to Iraq and Afghanistan. In the 2010 Quadrennial Diplomacy and Development Review, State noted that an expeditionary capacity to address complex conflicts and crises must become part of the "new normal" for the department and its personnel.[1]

Over the years, State has relied heavily on contractors to help accomplish its missions in both Iraq and Afghanistan. For example, State's reported obligations on contracts to help it carry out its missions in Iraq and Afghanistan were a combined $2.8 billion in fiscal year 2011 alone, representing 30 percent of its total contract obligations worldwide. Of the approximately 16,000 personnel State had planned as of summer 2011 to constitute the U.S. mission in Iraq, about 14,000 were contractors. In Afghanistan, the planned U.S. diplomatic presence after the realignment of DOD forces in 2014 is expected to include approximately 4,400 personnel, of which approximately 2,700 would be contractors.

---

[1]The Quadrennial Diplomacy and Development Review is an assessment by State and the U.S. Agency for International Development on how those two agencies can become more efficient, accountable, and effective in light of new threats and opportunities. It provides a blueprint for elevating American "civilian power" to better advance U.S. national interests and to be a better partner to the U.S. military. U.S. Department of State, *Leading through Civilian Power, The First Quadrennial Diplomacy and Development Review* (Washington, D.C.: 2010).

Contractors are working to support the U.S. diplomatic presence in both countries, but not all of them are working under contracts awarded and administered by State. Instead, State has turned to DOD to acquire some critical goods and services through interagency acquisitions—also known as interagency contracting.

Interagency acquisitions, such as State's use of DOD's acquisition assistance, can provide a number of benefits to agencies, including to help them streamline the procurement process, leverage unique expertise in a particular type of procurement, and achieve savings. However, such acquisitions also pose a variety of risks. GAO has designated the management of interagency contracting as a high risk area since 2005, in part because of the need for stronger internal controls, clear definitions of roles and responsibilities, and training to ensure proper use of this contracting method.[2] To this end, federal acquisition regulation and guidance require, among other things, that agencies carefully consider whether an interagency acquisition is a sound business decision and formally document the terms and conditions in an interagency agreement.[3]

The risks of interagency acquisitions are compounded by the challenges of contracting in environments such as Iraq and Afghanistan. The Commission on Wartime Contracting in Iraq and Afghanistan noted in its final report that interagency coordination requires "clear delineation of roles and responsibilities … effective interagency processes, and sufficient staff to perform the coordination tasks," while also noting that "the volume and complexity of contract actions have overwhelmed the ability of government to plan for, manage, and oversee contractors."[4] We have previously reported on State's challenges with both interagency acquisitions and contracting in Iraq and Afghanistan. For example, we reported in 2008 that State had limited insights into its use of interagency acquisitions, including those with performance in Iraq, which hindered

---

[2]GAO, *High-Risk Series: An Update,* GAO-05-207 (Washington, D.C.: January 2005).

[3]Federal Acquisition Regulation (FAR) §17.502 and Office of Management and Budget (OMB), Office of Federal Procurement Policy, *Improving the Management and Use of Interagency Acquisitions* (Washington, D.C.: June 6, 2008).

[4]Commission on Wartime Contracting in Iraq and Afghanistan, *Transforming Wartime Contracting: Controlling Costs, Reducing Risks, Final Report to Congress* (Arlington, VA Aug. 31, 2011).

contract oversight.[5] In reports issued annually since 2008, we consistently found that State lacked reliable sources and methods to report on its contracts and contractor personnel in Iraq and Afghanistan.[6] Further, we reported in 2010 that State did not always provide enhanced oversight as required for certain contracts in Iraq and Afghanistan, despite the potential for loss of government control and accountability for mission-related policy and program decisions.[7]

Because of broad congressional interest in U.S. efforts in Iraq and Afghanistan, we performed our work under the authority of the Comptroller General of the United States to conduct work on his own initiative. In this report, to better understand how State is managing its increased responsibilities for the missions in Iraq and Afghanistan with respect to the acquisition of critical goods and services, we evaluated (1) the nature and extent of State's reliance on DOD for the acquisition of critical goods and services, (2) factors that contributed to this reliance, and (3) whether State and DOD are making and implementing decisions regarding this reliance consistent with regulation and guidance.

To describe the nature and extent of State's reliance on DOD for the acquisition of critical goods and services in Iraq and Afghanistan, we reviewed documentation, including lists of contracts supporting State's presence in the two countries, agency correspondence, interagency acquisition agreements, memorandums of understanding and agreement, and other authorizations to use DOD resources. We also interviewed State and DOD officials in the United States, Iraq, and Afghanistan responsible for acquisition activities. For Iraq, our scope was limited to

---

[5]GAO, *Interagency Contracting: Need for Improved Information and Policy Implementation at the Department of State*, GAO-08-578 (Washington, D.C.: May 8, 2008).

[6]See GAO, *Iraq and Afghanistan: DOD, State, and USAID Cannot Fully Account for Contracts, Assistance Instruments, and Associated Personnel*, GAO-11-886 (Washington, D.C.: Sept. 15, 2011); *Iraq and Afghanistan: DOD, State, and USAID Face Continued Challenges in Tracking Contracts, Assistance Instruments, and Associated Personnel*, GAO-11-1 (Washington, D.C.: Oct. 1, 2010); *Contingency Contracting: DOD, State, and USAID Continue to Face Challenges in Tracking Contractor Personnel and Contracts in Iraq and Afghanistan*, GAO-10-1 (Washington, D.C.: Oct. 1, 2009); and *Contingency Contracting: DOD, State, and USAID Contracts and Contractor Personnel in Iraq and Afghanistan*, GAO-09-19 (Washington, D.C.: Oct. 1, 2008).

[7]GAO, *Contingency Contracting: Improvements Needed in Management of Contractors Supporting Contract and Grant Administration in Iraq and Afghanistan*, GAO-10-357 (Washington, D.C.: Apr. 12, 2010).

those critical goods and services supporting State's assumption of responsibility to lead the U.S. mission. For Afghanistan, we limited our scope to services for which State relied on DOD for the acquisition of critical services at the time of our review and reviewed the one associated contract and task order. We identified a subset of 22 acquisitions for which DOD performed one or more of the steps in the acquisition process. Among these, we identified 20 assisted interagency acquisitions, including some for Iraq that State requested of DOD beginning in April 2010.[8]

To identify factors that contributed to reliance, we reviewed State and DOD transition planning documents for Iraq and Afghanistan and interviewed State and DOD officials regarding rationales for reliance on DOD. On the basis of the information obtained through these documents and interviews, we collected detailed data on the composition of State's acquisition workforce and processes State uses to develop its workforce. We compared these data and processes to acquisition activities, personnel, and expertise that ultimately were needed to acquire critical goods and services in Iraq. We also compared State's processes for developing its workforce—including using a working capital fund to increase staff—with its own planned improvements and with practices for assessing performance of working capital funds.

To determine whether State is making decisions regarding its reliance on DOD for the acquisition of critical goods and services and both departments are implementing these decisions consistent with regulation and guidance, we reviewed documentation of coordination and decision making since April 2010 related to Iraq. We also interviewed State and DOD officials in the United States, Iraq, and Afghanistan. To determine how State made decisions to rely on interagency acquisitions with DOD, we compared documentation on coordination, assessment, and approval of interagency acquisitions to Federal Acquisition Regulation (FAR) requirements and Office of Management and Budget (OMB) guidance for ensuring that an interagency acquisition is the best procurement approach and a sound business decision. To assess the departments' arrangements for implementing decisions to use interagency acquisitions, we compared agency documentation to FAR requirements and OMB

---

[8]An assisted acquisition is a type of interagency acquisition where a servicing agency performs acquisition activities on a requesting agency's behalf, such as awarding and administering a contract, task order, or delivery order. FAR § 2.101.

guidance for having written agreements for assisted interagency acquisitions, including certain features of those agreements. We also compared payment arrangements and activities between State and DOD with respect to the interagency acquisitions with the statutory requirement under the Economy Act for payment on the basis of actual costs.[9] To identify State's efforts to determine whether it should continue to rely on DOD contracts, we reviewed available documentation on existing interagency acquisitions and interviewed State and DOD officials responsible for acquisition planning activities. We then compared these efforts with the FAR requirements and OMB guidance on interagency acquisitions and regulations on acquisition planning.

We conducted this performance audit from March 2011 to August 2012 in accordance with generally accepted government auditing standards. Those standards require that we plan and perform the audit to obtain sufficient, appropriate evidence to provide a reasonable basis for our findings and conclusions based on our audit objectives. We believe that the evidence obtained provides a reasonable basis for our findings and conclusions based on our audit objectives.

Background

State's Presence in Iraq and Afghanistan

The Security Agreement between the United States and the Government of Iraq directed that DOD was to complete the withdrawal of forces and transition the lead role for a fully diplomatic U.S. presence in Iraq to State by December 31, 2011.[10] As we reported in September 2011, for DOD to focus on the final drawdown phase, DOD had set a condition that State become "mission capable" for its civilian-led presence in Iraq by

---

[9] 31 U.S.C. § 1535; FAR § 17.502-2(d). The Economy Act provides general authority for federal agencies to undertake interagency acquisitions when a more specific statutory authority does not exist.

[10] *Agreement on the Withdrawal of United States Forces from Iraq and the Organization of Their Activities during Their Temporary Presence in Iraq*, United States–Iraq, art. 24, para. 1 (Nov. 17, 2008).

October 1, 2011.[11] State determined that to reach independent mission capability, each of its sites throughout the country must have:

- secure and protected facilities,
- secure ground and air movement,
- quick reaction capability,
- communications,
- medical care and evacuation, and
- infrastructure and life support.[12]

Prior to the withdrawal of U.S. forces from Iraq, DOD had provided many of the critical goods and services State needed to support its missions. Although State had responsibility for providing some services to its own personnel, DOD personnel and contractors had been providing basic life support services, medical services, and Iraq-wide security capabilities and infrastructure. For example, while State had a single health unit providing primary care at the embassy, DOD had responsibility for emergency care as well as medical evacuation. In addition, State had a contracted embassy guard force and provided for movement security of its own personnel using contractors but relied on DOD for general security across the country. Military forces provided theater security, operating a range of technologies such as unmanned aerial vehicles (UAV) for intelligence, surveillance, and reconnaissance; radars to detect and warn of incoming rocket and mortar attacks; and systems to help conduct background investigations on local national staff and contractors. Further, leading up to the transition of responsibility to State, a wide range of basic support services, including dining, laundry, and waste management, had been provided to U.S. government and contractor personnel through DOD contracts, including the Army's Logistics Civil

---

[11]GAO, *Iraq Drawdown: Opportunities Exist to Improve Equipment Visibility, Contractor Demobilization, and Clarity of Post-2011 DOD Role*, GAO-11-774 (Washington, D.C.: Sept. 16, 2011).

[12]As of June 2012, this exclusively diplomatic presence consisted of 14 sites: 8 maintained by State for diplomatic purposes and 6 additional sites maintained by DOD (5 for the Office of Security Cooperation-Iraq, and 1 for the Office of Security Cooperation-Iraq and State's consulate in Kirkuk), which is managing security assistance and cooperation with the Government of Iraq. For additional information on the status of establishing support at these sites, see GAO, *Mission Iraq: State and DOD Face Challenges in Finalizing Support and Security Capabilities*, GAO-12-856T (Washington, D.C.: June 28, 2012).

Augmentation Program (LOGCAP) contract. Several LOGCAP task orders supported State's needs at the embassy.[13]

With the withdrawal of U.S. military forces from Iraq in December 2011, State would become solely responsible in January 2012 for supporting its presence throughout the country. To ensure goods and services were in place for the transition of responsibility to State, acquisition activities—such as planning, defining requirements, developing cost estimates, and preparing solicitations—needed to occur for each of the critical goods and services in advance. In 2010, as the departments' planning for DOD's withdrawal and transition to a State-led presence in Iraq got underway, and throughout the following year, security conditions were such that State's traditional means of ensuring basic services in posts around the world—relying on the local economy—were not available, and State's security capabilities were insufficient to support the planned presence. Senior DOD and State officials have acknowledged that coordination occurred late in the process and the delays made the transition more challenging.[14] Adding to the challenge was uncertainty as to whether DOD would reach agreement with the Government of Iraq for a follow-on presence of U.S. military forces, which would also have required support services if agreed to. To help State identify critical requirements for which it had previously relied on DOD and address other issues associated with the transition, the two departments established an Executive Steering Group cochaired by the Deputy Assistant Secretaries for Program Support (DOD) and Logistics Management (State) in September 2010. The group proposed solutions to fulfill State's requirements, including acquisition of needed capabilities through a combination of State acquisitions and interagency acquisitions with DOD under the authority of the Economy Act, as well as equipment transfers from DOD. The group received guidance from the Principal Deputy Under Secretary of Defense for Acquisition, Technology, and Logistics and the Under Secretary of State for Management.

In Afghanistan, State and DOD currently share responsibility for the U.S. presence. State's presence includes the U.S. embassy in Kabul and regional consulates, as well as civilian personnel assigned to locations

---

[13]A task order is an order for services placed against an established contract or with government sources. FAR § 2.101.

[14]GAO-11-774.

throughout Afghanistan. State currently provides security for its own facilities and personnel, although DOD continues to provide for countrywide security. Current U.S. strategy calls for provinces and districts to transition to greater Afghan government control as local capacity improves and conditions allow.[15] Further, the United States, along with its North Atlantic Treaty Organization partners, has committed to fully transferring lead security responsibility to the Afghan government by the end of 2014. In May 2012, a United States-Afghanistan Strategic Partnership Agreement was signed that provides for the possibility of U.S. forces in Afghanistan after 2014, to be determined in a follow-on bilateral security agreement.[16] As the United States plans for a reduction in U.S. forces, State is making plans for realignment of its diplomatic enduring presence to meet policy objectives.

Interagency Acquisitions

An interagency acquisition takes place when an agency needing supplies or services (the requesting agency) obtains them from another agency (the servicing agency). The term includes interagency acquisitions under the Economy Act and non-Economy Act acquisitions completed under other statutory authority.[17] Statutory authority, such as the Economy Act, is required for federal agencies to conduct interagency acquisitions to avoid running afoul of federal fiscal law.[18] The Economy Act provides general authority for federal agencies to undertake interagency acquisitions when a more specific statutory authority does not exist. Interagency acquisitions authorized by the Economy Act can save the government duplicative effort and costs when appropriately used. Circumstances under which an Economy Act interagency acquisition may be appropriately used include when one agency already has a contract

---

[15]The U.S. strategy for Afghanistan refers to the strategy announced in a March 2009 speech by the President, which was reiterated in a December 2010 strategic review.

[16]*Enduring Strategic Partnership Agreement*, United States–Afghanistan, § III, para. 6, (May 2, 2012).

[17]Economy Act of 1932, 31 U.S.C. § 1535; FAR § 17.502-2.

[18]Fiscal law provides that an agency generally must use its appropriated funds for the purposes for which the appropriations were made. 31 U.S.C. § 1301(a). In addition, an agency receiving goods or services funded by another agency's appropriations must reimburse the servicing agency to avoid improperly augmenting the requesting agency's appropriations. Furthermore, payments received by the servicing agency for goods or services provided, without other statutory authority, must be deposited into the Treasury as miscellaneous receipts. 31 U.S.C. § 3302(b).

for goods or services similar to those needed by another agency or when an agency has unique capabilities or expertise that qualify it to enter into a contract.

State has its own policy for making and implementing decisions regarding the use of interagency acquisitions. In 2002, before the risks associated with interagency acquisition were widely reported, State implemented the State First policy for acquisition that directs State's domestic bureaus and offices to use State contracting offices, as opposed to paying another agency to conduct an acquisition, unless the appropriate State acquisition and procurement policy officials grant a waiver. In April 2008, State updated its State First policy noting that GAO, State's Inspector General, and OMB had all identified the interagency acquisition process as an area of high risk requiring active management. In doing so, State implemented GAO recommendations to strengthen and clarify the policy by updating it to cover a wider range of interagency acquisitions and to require that when requesting a waiver, a bureau identify a contracting officer's representative (COR) who would provide technical oversight of the interagency acquisition.

As part of the Duncan Hunter National Defense Authorization Act for Fiscal Year 2009, Congress enacted section 865 on preventing abuse of interagency acquisitions, which resulted in OMB's issuance of comprehensive guidance in June 2008 and revisions to the FAR in 2010.[19] OMB's guidance recognized the risks of interagency acquisitions, noting that "[l]ack of clear lines of responsibility between agencies with requirements (requesting agencies) and the agencies which provide acquisition support and award contracts on their behalf (servicing agencies) has contributed to inadequate planning, inconsistent use of competition, weak contract management, and concerns regarding financial controls."[20] The guidance directed agencies to

- ensure the use of an interagency acquisition is a sound business decision by requiring consideration of certain factors and
- strengthen the management of assisted interagency acquisitions by requiring formal agreements between requesting and servicing

[19]Pub. L. No. 110-417, § 865 (2008).

[20]OMB, Office of Federal Procurement Policy, *Improving the Management and Use of Interagency Acquisitions* (Washington, D.C.: June 6, 2008).

agencies that contain certain elements, such as roles and responsibilities for acquisition activities.

The FAR's requirements for interagency acquisitions were amended in 2010, as directed by Congress, and reflect the 2008 OMB guidance. Under the FAR, agencies are to determine an interagency acquisition is the best procurement approach among alternative procurement approaches through a determination that an interagency acquisition

- satisfies the requesting agency's schedule, performance, and delivery requirements (taking into account the servicing agency's authority, experience, and expertise as well as customer satisfaction with the servicing agency's past performance),
- is cost-effective (taking into account reasonableness of the servicing agency's fees), and
- will result in the use of funds in accordance with appropriation limitations and compliance with the requesting agency's laws and policies.[21]

In addition, for assisted interagency acquisitions, the FAR requires that the servicing agency and requesting agency sign a written interagency agreement, which establishes the general terms and conditions governing the relationship, and that they refer to the OMB guidance in preparing these agreements.[22]

Support provided by one agency to another can span across the acquisition cycle, including acquisition planning, contract award, contract management, and contract oversight (see figure 1).

---

[21]FAR §17.502-1(a)(1).

[22]FAR §17.502-1(b).

Figure 1: Phases of the Acquisition Process and Associated Activities

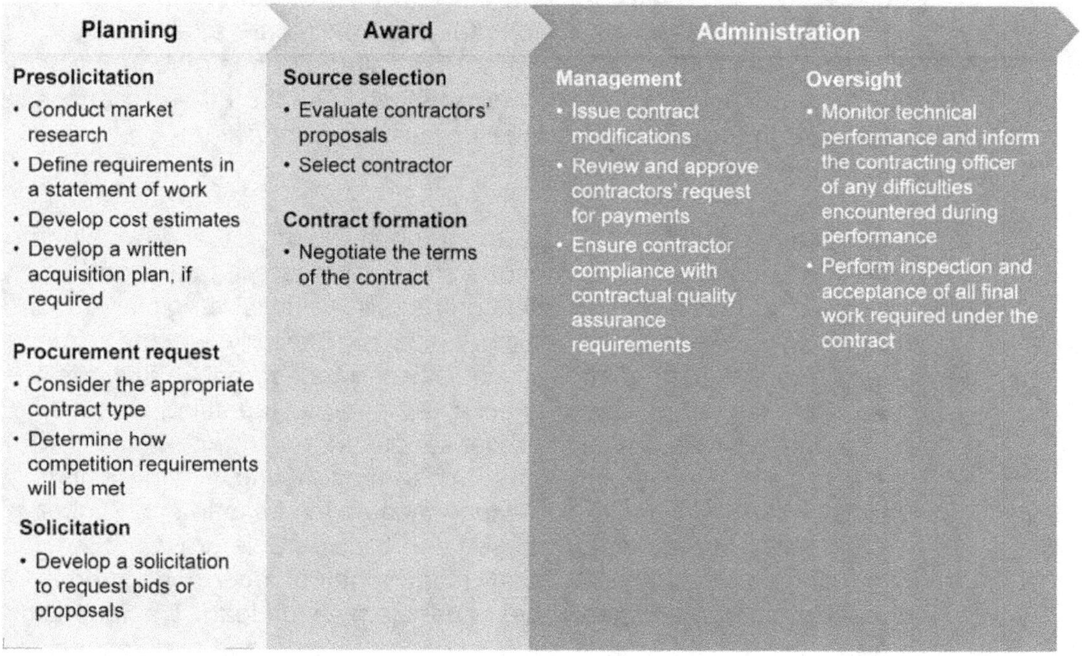

Planning	Award	Administration	
Presolicitation	**Source selection**	**Management**	**Oversight**
• Conduct market research	• Evaluate contractors' proposals	• Issue contract modifications	• Monitor technical performance and inform the contracting officer of any difficulties encountered during performance
• Define requirements in a statement of work	• Select contractor	• Review and approve contractors' request for payments	
• Develop cost estimates	**Contract formation**	• Ensure contractor compliance with contractual quality assurance requirements	• Perform inspection and acceptance of all final work required under the contract
• Develop a written acquisition plan, if required	• Negotiate the terms of the contract		
Procurement request			
• Consider the appropriate contract type			
• Determine how competition requirements will be met			
Solicitation			
• Develop a solicitation to request bids or proposals			

Source: GAO analysis of the Federal Acquisition Regulation.

Acquisition Management Structure and Challenges at State

Responsibility for acquisition policy and management at State is shared by two offices within the Bureau of Administration—the Office of the Procurement Executive (OPE) and the Office of Acquisitions Management (AQM). For example, OPE is responsible for establishing acquisition policy, such as the State First policy that AQM is to implement with OPE's concurrence through waivers or exceptions to that policy. Other OPE responsibilities include prescribing and implementing acquisition policies, regulations, and procedures; managing State's procurement reporting system; appointing contracting officers; establishing a system for measuring the performance of State contracting offices; and managing the acquisition career program to improve the competence of the department's acquisition workforce. AQM is responsible for providing a full range of contracting services to support activities across State, including acquisition planning, contract negotiations, cost and price analysis, and contract administration. AQM is responsible for over 98 percent of State's acquisitions. State's Under Secretary for Management has overall responsibility for AQM, OPE, and the functional bureaus that have requirements for contracted services in Iraq and Afghanistan. These functional bureaus include Diplomatic Security, which is State's security and law enforcement arm, and the Office of Medical Services, which provides health care at embassies worldwide. The Under Secretary for Political Affairs has responsibility for identifying the needs for goods and services to support the presences in Iraq and Afghanistan through the Bureaus of Near Eastern Affairs and South and Central Asian Affairs, respectively.

State acknowledged in its 2010 Quadrennial Diplomacy and Development Review that it needed to change the way it awards, manages, and monitors contracts to ensure that contracts serve its strategic interests and deliver results for the American taxpayer. Similarly, we and others have reported on long-standing acquisition management challenges at State. For example, State's Inspector General has identified contracting and procurement as one of the most serious management and performance challenges facing the department, noting with particular concern that AQM continues to experience an increase in the number of procurement transactions processed and considerable growth in the dollar value of procurement actions issued without a corresponding increase in contracting personnel to handle the workload. The Inspector General found that frequent turnover of contract support staff, especially overseas, has resulted in waste, a lack of adequate coordination, and a loss of institutional memory and that his office has identified several instances in which contract administration and oversight were not adequate, including in Iraq and Afghanistan.

State Has Relied Heavily on DOD for the Acquisition of Critical Goods and Services

To help State meet its requirements for critical goods and services in Iraq and Afghanistan, DOD supported State on 22 acquisitions, as shown in table 1.

Table 1: State and DOD Roles in Acquisitions of Critical Goods and Services Currently Supporting the U.S. Missions in Iraq and Afghanistan

Critical service	Acquisitions (number)	Contract value (dollars in millions)[a]	Roles in acquisition activities			
					Administration	
			Planning	Award	Management	Oversight
Iraq						
Basic services/goods	Logistics Civil Augmentation Program (1)	$506.5	●	●	●	◉
	Food and Fuel (7)	273.0[b]	◉	●	●	◉
Security	Security Support Services-Iraq (2)	73.0	●	●	●	◉
	Theater Wide Internal Security Services (5)	20.1	●	●	●	◉
	Sense and Warn (2)	74.1	●	●	●	◉
	Field and Installation Readiness Support Team Maintenance (1)	37.4	◉	●	●	●
	Vetting Services (1)	7.0	◉	●	●	○
	Unmanned Aerial Vehicles (1)	28.0	◉	○	○	○
Medical	Medical Support Services-Iraq (1)	467.5	◉	○	○	○
Afghanistan						
Basic services	Logistics Civil Augmentation Program (1)	6.9	●	●	●	●

Legend: ● DOD lead
○ State lead
◉ Shared responsibility

Source: GAO analysis of State and DOD contract documentation, data, and discussion with officials.

[a]Contract value, for the purpose of this table, is the estimated value at award plus priced options and modifications as of April 30, 2012.

[b]These DOD supply contracts serve multiple agencies, so we report State's total estimated cost per fiscal year, including direct costs and overhead, not value as of April 30, 2012.

DOD awarded and managed 20 interagency acquisitions on State's behalf under the authority of the Economy Act with an estimated value of $1 billion for basic support services and goods as well as security services.[23] DOD also provided support on two State acquisitions for medical services and UAV operations. Across the 22 acquisitions, DOD has been involved in one or more aspects of the acquisition cycle, including planning, award, management, and oversight. Based on our review of documents and interviews with officials, we identified at least 128 DOD personnel with contracting and subject matter expertise who provided support for these acquisitions—46 in the United States and 82 in Iraq.

Of the 22 acquisitions, 20 were assisted acquisitions in which DOD executed one or more contract actions on State's behalf and had the lead in managing the contract.

- *Basic Services—Logistics Civil Augmentation Program (LOGCAP):* DOD's LOGCAP program office and Rock Island Contracting Center led planning, award, and management of a task order for basic services at multiple locations across Iraq. LOGCAP provides for a wide range of utilities and maintenance services including dining, laundry, and waste management. State participated in planning and leads contract oversight, with quality assurance support from the Defense Contract Management Agency (DCMA).[24] In Kabul, Afghanistan, DOD is performing all acquisition activities on State's behalf supporting its requirement for three dining facilities.
- *Basic Goods—Supplies of Food and Fuel:* The Defense Logistics Agency (DLA) awarded seven contracts for food and fuel that the LOGCAP contractors use to provide their services in Iraq. DLA is

---

[23]The 20 assisted interagency acquisitions include DOD contracts under which State is a customer, task orders awarded by DOD under DOD indefinite delivery / indefinite quantity contracts on behalf of State, and modifications to DOD contracts and task orders made on behalf of State. When the same DOD task order was modified multiple times on State's behalf, we counted the task order that was modified on State's behalf as one interagency acquisition and did not count each individual modification as a separate interagency acquisition.

[24]DCMA provides contract administration services such as quality assurance oversight, when delegated that authority by the contracting officer. DCMA has an organization dedicated to supporting contingency contracts. DCMA is responsible for ensuring the integrity of contractual processes and providing a broad range of contract management and administration services. We reported in November 2011 that, amid DCMA's ongoing efforts to rebuild its capacity, several factors presented challenges, including that officials believe contingency missions have a constraining effect on DCMA's domestic mission. GAO, *Defense Contract Management Agency: Amid Ongoing Efforts to Rebuild Capacity, Several Factors Present Challenges in Meeting Its Missions*, GAO-12-83 (Washington, D.C.: Nov. 3, 2011).

responsible for awarding the contracts, with DLA and State sharing planning and oversight responsibilities.

- *Security—Security Support Services-Iraq (SSS-I), Theater Wide Internal Security Services (TWISS), and Sense and Warn:* Multiple DOD contracting offices have taken actions to provide State with security capabilities in Iraq. The Rock Island Contracting Center led planning and award of two SSS-I task orders. The U.S. Central Command's (CENTCOM) Joint Theater Support Contracting Command modified five existing TWISS task orders for guard and movement security services.[25] DOD's Redstone Contracting Center and the Defense Information Technology Contracting Organization modified two existing Sense and Warn task orders for the installation and operation of a capability to detect incoming rocket, artillery, and mortar attacks. A DOD program office conducted a survey of State facilities in Iraq to determine Sense and Warn requirements. DOD and State share oversight responsibilities.
- *Security—Field and Installation Readiness Support Team (FIRST) Maintenance:* The Rock Island Contracting Center modified an existing task order to provide for maintenance of the Sense and Warn capability and biometrics equipment, as well as other DOD-loaned equipment. State participated in planning to meet its requirements, but DOD leads contract management and oversight.
- *Security—Vetting Services:* The Rock Island Contracting Center awarded a task order for additional screeners and counterintelligence specialists to support State's vetting of Iraqi nationals working under the LOGCAP contract. According to State officials, both State and DOD contributed to acquisition planning and oversight. DCMA manages the task order on State's behalf, while a State regional security officer serves as a COR to provide oversight.

Across all of these assisted acquisitions, in addition to DCMA's contract management support, the Defense Contract Audit Agency (DCAA) provides audit support.[26]

---

[25]State independently planned and awarded four task orders under its Worldwide Protective Services contracts to provide security for its facilities and personnel in Iraq, and its personnel are responsible for contract management and oversight. However, when mobilization of State's Worldwide Protective Services contractors was delayed, State requested that DOD extend performance under its TWISS task orders at five locations throughout Iraq to ensure continuation of critical security services.

[26]DCAA provides accounting and financial advisory services for DOD in connection with the negotiation, administration, and settlement of contracts and subcontracts. DCAA also provides contract audit services to other federal government agencies as appropriate.

State independently awarded and administers two of the acquisitions we reviewed, with DOD providing acquisition planning support in both cases:

- *Unmanned Aerial Vehicles:* State's decision to operate UAVs in Iraq led it to independently award, manage, and oversee its first contract for UAV operations and maintenance after DOD assisted in market research and requirements definition.
- *Medical Support Services-Iraq:* Contracting for medical services on such a large scale was a new and unfamiliar task to State. However, it independently awarded and manages its own contract for primary and emergency medical care to State personnel and some contractors. DOD's medical command officials assisted with requirements development, and DOD personnel participated as nonvoting members on the technical panel evaluating contractor proposals.

State's Reliance on DOD to Respond to Urgent Requirements Stemmed from Limitations in Its Acquisition Workforce Capacity That Persist

In justifying its 2010 requests for support from DOD in acquiring critical goods and services, State cited the urgency of ensuring requirements were met as the U.S. military withdrew from Iraq. Underlying that sense of urgency was the insufficient capacity and expertise of State's acquisition workforce. Specifically, State and DOD concluded that State lacked sufficient personnel, both in numbers and expertise, to conduct acquisition activities and that it did not have the requisite time to increase workforce capacity required to have contracts in place following the transition. State has taken some steps to address the acquisition workforce challenges that prompted it to seek DOD's assistance by increasing the number of acquisition professionals. However, State has not fully assessed whether (1) the effort to increase its acquisition workforce is sufficient to meet surge requirements, (2) its acquisition workforce has the proper skill and government/contractor mix, and (3) it has sufficient numbers of qualified oversight personnel to support its own contracting efforts in Iraq and Afghanistan in the future. For example, State's workforce planning through 2014 does not address specific needs for contract oversight personnel to support complex acquisitions in environments like Iraq or Afghanistan, even though DOD expects State to assume additional oversight responsibilities at the start of 2014.

Requirements to Acquire Goods and Services for Iraq Exceeded Capacity and Expertise of State's Acquisition Workforce

State lacked sufficient personnel, both in terms of numbers and expertise, to conduct acquisition activities. State was not able to increase its capacity in time to support the transition to a State-led civilian presence. In the justification accompanying the Under Secretary of State for Management's April 2010 request for the continued use of LOGCAP,

State noted that (1) if it was not able to rely on LOGCAP, it would be forced to redirect its resources to develop, implement, and oversee a new basic support infrastructure throughout the country and (2) doing so would place the civilian presence at risk given the magnitude, uncertainties, and complexities involved. State had explored awarding its own contract for its post-2011 support services as an alternative, but discontinued the effort in June 2010, in part because it could not develop its contract management and oversight capabilities quickly enough. In August 2010, after an assessment of the critical support needs in Iraq, DOD concluded that State's organizational shortfalls in contracting placed the transition at a potential for significant risk if State had to assume responsibility for independently contracting for basic support services. The following month DOD agreed to provide the requested support to prevent mission degradation.

For most of the 22 acquisitions we reviewed, State did not have the contracting or subject matter expertise necessary to plan, manage, or oversee the contracts, so the department sought DOD personnel's expertise. For example, when State requested DOD's assistance for the continuation of DOD's LOGCAP and associated food and fuel contracts to support establishing an exclusively diplomatic presence, State recognized that it did not have the sufficient experience and expertise to perform the necessary contract oversight. LOGCAP provides for dining and laundry service as well as light construction, comprehensive utilities services (power, water, sewage, fuel, and waste management), airfield operations (including air traffic control), ground transportation and vehicle maintenance, and shipping and receiving. A senior State official explained to us that DCMA assistance was needed to help oversee this wide range of services, in part because State personnel are not accustomed to overseeing, for example, dining facilities or power plants. A comparison of DOD and State contracting and oversight personnel supporting the award, administration, and oversight of State's LOGCAP task order in Iraq illustrates the extent of State's personnel shortfalls. As shown in figure 2, DOD provided 71 contracting and oversight personnel over the acquisition cycle to support this task order, while State provided fewer than 20 oversight personnel.

Figure 2: DOD and State Contracting and Oversight Personnel Involved in the Planning, Award, and Oversight of the LOGCAP Task Order Supporting State in Iraq

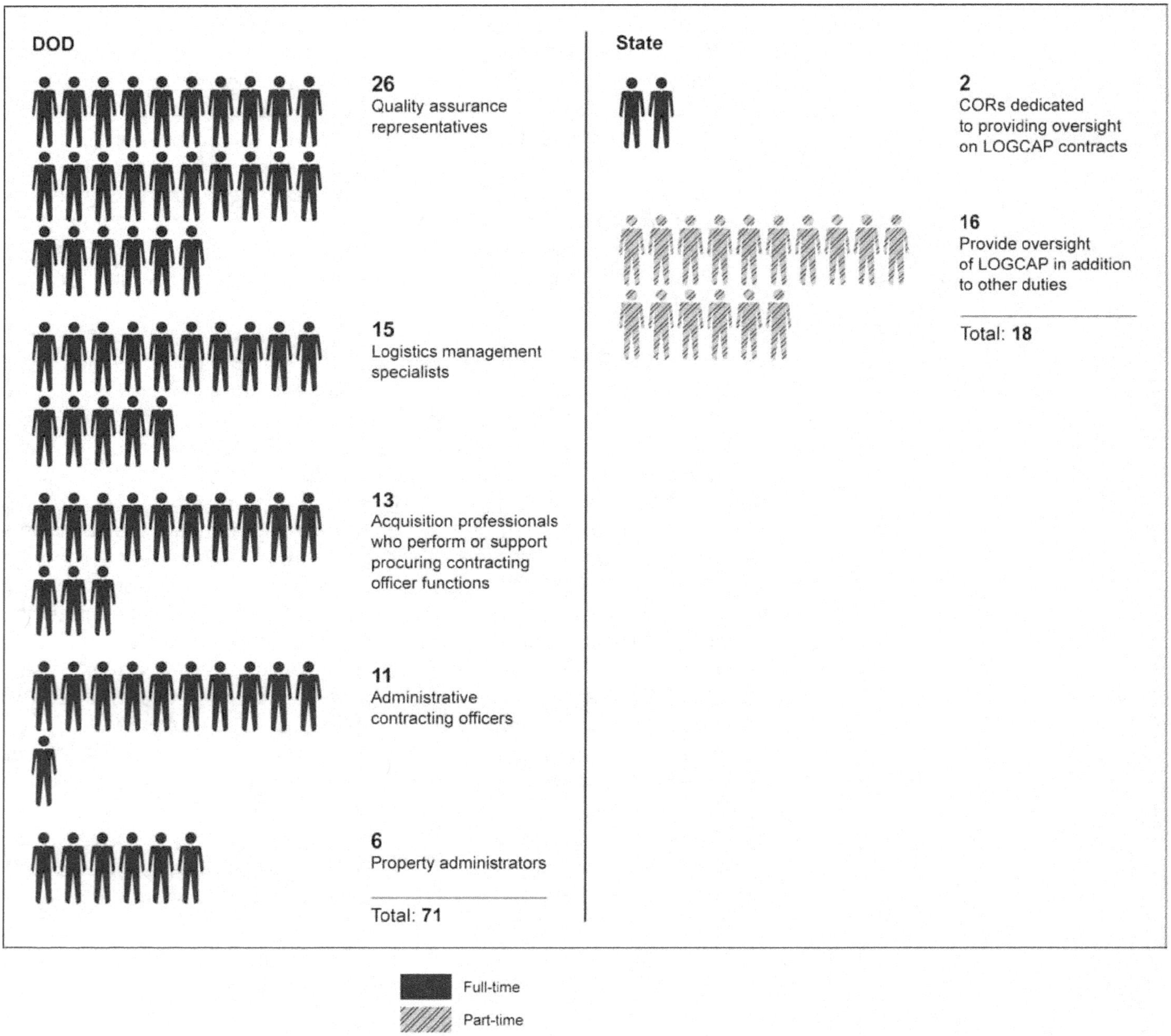

DOD

26
Quality assurance representatives

15
Logistics management specialists

13
Acquisition professionals who perform or support procuring contracting officer functions

11
Administrative contracting officers

6
Property administrators

Total: **71**

State

2
CORs dedicated to providing oversight on LOGCAP contracts

16
Provide oversight of LOGCAP in addition to other duties

Total: **18**

■ Full-time

▨ Part-time

Source: GAO analysis of State and DOD data.

In addition, when developing its own contract for medical support services, State relied on DOD medical planning experts in Iraq in part because of DOD's expertise operating in a conflict environment. State's medical officials tasked with developing the requirements informed us that they were not prepared to write requirements for the medical services contract on their own because they had little to no experience related to contracting. Further, they stated that no one within AQM could assist them because State did not have contracting personnel with expertise related to medical services.

State Has Not Fully Addressed Factors That Contributed to Reliance on DOD Acquisition Support

State Has Not Assessed Whether the Effort to Increase Its Acquisition Workforce Is Sufficient

State has taken some steps to address its long-standing shortage of acquisition professionals by using a dedicated source of funding for its acquisition workforce. Until 2008, AQM's operations were funded by annual appropriations, which State acquisition officials believed did not provide a basis to obtain sufficient government or contractor personnel. In 2008, AQM began using a working capital fund—a shared services model that provides procurement services on a fee-for-service basis to both domestic and overseas customers.[27] A one percent fee is charged to State's internal customers, which is then used to finance all of AQM's operations, including salaries and travel. According to State AQM officials, State began using the fund because it needed to be able to quickly respond to acquisition workload increases—including those specifically associated with operations in Iraq—and the fund would generate a volume of resources directly proportional to AQM's workload.

State's expectation that the working capital fund would allow AQM to be more responsive to increased demands on its acquisition workforce has been partially met. Between February 2008, when AQM began using the working capital fund, and April 2010, when State requested DOD's support for acquisitions in Iraq, AQM added 21 full-time government personnel and 60 support contractors. By February 2012, shortly after

---

[27]22 U.S.C. § 2684.

State took lead responsibility in Iraq, AQM added 25 more staff. This represents a 59 percent increase in AQM's workforce overall since the implementation of the fund in 2008 (see table 2).

Table 2: Number of Personnel in AQM from 2008 to 2012

	February 2008	April 2010	February 2012
Number of government personnel	141	162	200
Number of contract support staff	39	99	86
Total	**180**	**261**	**286**

Source: State data.

Even with these increases, State's Inspector General reported in November 2010 and 2011 that the department lacked sufficient contracting personnel to handle the increase in the number of procurement transactions processed and the rise in the dollar value of procurement actions issued over the past decade. The Inspector General also identified associated challenges in acquisition planning, administration, and oversight in places like Iraq. Further, the relationship at State between procurement obligations and the number of government contracting professionals—a ratio that State has used to track its progress towards the goal of eliminating its long-standing shortage of acquisition professionals—worsened from 2008 to 2010. Over the two years, this ratio rose from about $47 million per government contracting professional in 2008 to about $57 million in 2010.[28] In 2010, the department assessed its 2008 ratio as unfavorable compared with that of other federal agencies, but it has not established the target ratio it hopes to achieve.

State has not assessed how well the working capital fund has met expectations to surge the workforce for situations like Iraq and Afghanistan. State established the fund's one percent fee after assessing AQM's expenses in 2007, and according to officials, anticipated demands for an increase in contract services for Iraq. While State's Under

---

[28]State calculates a procurement ratio by dividing procurement obligations by the number of government employees classified in the General Schedule Contracting series (GS-1102). The GS-1102 series is important for federal agencies because these personnel develop the knowledge of the legislation, regulations, and methods of federal contracting and skills to conduct central acquisition responsibilities such as to manage, supervise, perform, or develop policies and procedures for procurement.

Secretary for Management has repeatedly testified that the fund is helping State to "surge" its resources to respond to contingency requirements, State has not assessed the extent to which the fund has helped AQM's workforce surge to meet requirements for Iraq and Afghanistan. In an April 2012 assessment of the fund, State identified some improvements as a result of its use of the fund, such as hiring additional staff that allowed for overall faster processing of contract actions, but did not address whether the fund has enabled AQM to surge its acquisition workforce capacity. This lack of an assessment of the fund's ability to help AQM respond to contingency requirements is inconsistent with our prior conclusions that agencies should establish performance measures for working capital funds that align with strategic goals.[29]

State Has Not Assessed the Skills and Workforce Mix Needed to Meet Future Requirements

Although State has acknowledged a shortage of contracting and subject-matter expertise in its requests for DOD's support in acquiring critical goods and services, the department has not assessed the expertise needed to support future contracting operations in Iraq and Afghanistan as part of its acquisition workforce planning efforts. We have previously reported that understanding where workforce gaps exist in the competencies and skills required to meet programmatic goals is key to helping agencies develop effective workforce strategies.[30] State's acquisition workforce human capital plan for fiscal years 2010 through 2014 does not address the need for additional skills or expertise for contracting personnel or subject-matter experts to support contracts in complex acquisition environments such as Iraq or Afghanistan.

State also has not fully leveraged DOD's expertise to further build its own capacity for managing complex acquisitions in environments like Iraq. For example, according to DOD and State officials, prior to the award of the LOGCAP task order, a State official from the embassy in Baghdad was working with contracting personnel at the Rock Island Contracting Center

---

[29]GAO, *Department of Justice: Working Capital Fund Adheres to Some Key Operating Principles but Could Better Measure Performance and Communicate with Customers*, GAO-12-289 (Washington, D.C.: Jan. 20, 2012); and *Intergovernmental Revolving Funds: Commerce Departmental and Census Working Capital Funds Should Better Reflect Key Operating Principles*, GAO-12-56 (Washington, D.C.: Nov. 18, 2011).

[30]GAO, *Department of Homeland Security: A Strategic Approach Is Needed to Better Ensure the Acquisition Workforce Can Meet Mission Needs*, GAO-09-30 (Washington, D.C.: Nov. 19, 2008).

to facilitate the refinement of requirements and source selection process. However, according to Rock Island Contracting Center officials responsible for planning and awarding the task order, State's AQM officials had minimal involvement in these activities, which limited their opportunities to gain insight and expertise. While State AQM officials are working with personnel at the embassy in Baghdad to identify continuing requirements beyond LOGCAP, DOD officials told us and State officials confirmed as of April 2012, AQM personnel were not working directly with their DOD counterparts at the Rock Island Contracting Center to build expertise even though State anticipates taking over the contracting function for these services within the next few years. State officials explained that there are no unique functions or processes for contracting in contingency environments such as Iraq and Afghanistan and, therefore, State does not need to develop a separate workforce expertise or capability for its efforts in those countries.

Approximately half of the personnel added to AQM's workforce since 2008 are support contractors. While we did not assess the specific roles being performed by these contractors, some of them may be performing contract administration functions. However, State has not assessed the extent to which it is appropriate for contractors to perform contract administration functions, which we recommended in April 2010 the department do.[31] As of February 2012, these support contractors accounted for approximately one-third of AQM's staff. State's Office of Inspector General attributed the increased reliance on contractors in part to delays and other difficulties associated with the hiring process for government employees, citing lead times of up to 18 months to hire government personnel. While contractors provide valuable support, they do not have the authority to perform certain types of acquisition activities such as awarding contracts or approving contractual documents. Moreover, State's Deputy Inspector General testified in April 2012 that the use of contractors to supplement staffing in support of acquisition management has increased risk related to potential conflict of interest. Without determining the extent to which support contractors should perform contract administration functions, State is limited in its ability to ensure that it has sufficient government contracting personnel to meet future needs in Iraq and Afghanistan.

---

[31]GAO-10-357.

State Has Not Sufficiently Planned for Contract Oversight in Iraq and Afghanistan

State has not conducted the planning necessary to ensure it has sufficient contract oversight capacity for Iraq and Afghanistan in the future, even though it has acknowledged a lack of personnel with requisite experience and expertise to meet its current oversight needs. Contract oversight was in State's scope of planned activities in Iraq, but the extent of planning for oversight functions was inconsistent among contracted services we reviewed. To carry out contract oversight, State generally relies on CORs appointed from programs within the department's regional and functional bureaus to help ensure that the contractor accomplishes the required work. These CORs are funded through programmatic and bureau budgets, as opposed to AQM's working capital fund. State typically assigns COR duties to staff whose primary duties are program management, so these staff perform COR duties part-time. The practice of having personnel perform their COR duties on a part-time basis is also used at other agencies, including DOD for its oversight of contracts in Iraq and Afghanistan. According to State contracting and regional bureau officials, State conducts general planning for CORs as part of the department's human capital planning process to meet its overall mission and generally determines the number of CORs necessary to oversee a specific contract during early acquisition planning meetings.

Because State officials had limited involvement in the acquisition planning, they did not have sufficient insight into the oversight required for basic support services in Iraq. According to DOD officials directly involved in the planning and award of the LOGCAP task order, State's limited involvement in acquisition planning led to State's difficulty in understanding the full extent of contract oversight needed. This included identifying the minimum number of CORs needed and their training. State's limited acquisition planning for the extent of oversight needed is reflected in State's fiscal year 2012 congressional budget justification, as well as State's fiscal year 2013 Mission and Strategic Resource Plan for the U.S. Mission to Iraq. In neither case did State identify funding or the number of personnel expected to perform contract oversight supporting the LOGCAP task order. It was only after extensive negotiation between State and DOD officials and the award of the LOGCAP task order that State agreed to assign the number of oversight personnel DOD considered sufficient. Providing the agreed upon level of oversight for the LOGCAP task order and other DOD awarded and managed contracts resulted in an unplanned allocation of staff for State. As a result of the negotiations with DCMA, State dedicated four of its personnel in Baghdad as full-time CORs rather than having them perform COR duties in addition to other responsibilities. Finally, even with new understanding of the level of contract oversight required for the LOGCAP task order, State's fiscal year 2013 congressional budget justification for Iraq does not request funding for additional positions to conduct oversight. As a result, State may need to again redirect personnel from other duties to perform as CORs for State's LOGCAP task order until its expiration at the end of 2013.

In contrast, State has improved its planning for contract oversight of private security contractors. We previously reported on improvements State made to its oversight of private security contractors in Iraq by increasing the number of diplomatic security personnel stationed in Iraq to oversee contractor activities and requesting and receiving funding to hire and train 100 additional agents.[32] To ensure it could sustain this progress, State conducted extensive planning to oversee its Worldwide Protective Services contract for guard and movement security services, which informed decisions to increase resources and personnel. For example, in 2010, State requested funding to add 15 full-time positions specifically for oversight of its worldwide personal protective services contracts. Similarly, for fiscal year 2011, State's Bureau of Diplomatic Security requested additional funding for costs associated with oversight personnel for contracts that provide protective security services throughout Iraq.

DOD documentation indicates an expectation that oversight and other acquisition support roles for basic support and other critical goods and services in Iraq should transition from DOD to State no later than the start of 2014. However, State has not determined its future requirements for oversight personnel and the funding needed to fulfill those needs. For example, State has not conducted an overall assessment of the number of personnel needed to replace DOD personnel conducting contract oversight on State's behalf in Iraq. Similarly, there has not been an assessment of the skills, expertise, and training such oversight personnel would need; whether other employees can be redirected to fulfill the oversight role; or requests for funding to ensure sufficient contract oversight capability for these contracts as they transition from DOD to State oversight. For example, State's Acquisition Workforce Human Capital Plan for Fiscal Years 2010 through 2014 does not address any specific needs for contract oversight personnel to support complex

---

[32]GAO, *Rebuilding Iraq: DOD and State Department Have Improved Oversight and Coordination of Private Security Contractors in Iraq, but Further Actions Are Needed to Sustain Improvements,* GAO-08-966 (Washington, D.C.: July 31, 2008).

acquisition environments such as Iraq or Afghanistan. Without conducting planning for contract oversight, State is not well positioned to determine whether it has sufficient time to hire or otherwise develop its capacity to meet future oversight needs or whether it again must rely on DOD to supplement its acquisition workforce. A decision to proceed with acquiring needed services without sufficient oversight personnel in place puts the agency at risk of being unable to identify and correct poor contractor performance in a timely manner and ensure consistent delivery of goods and services critical to maintaining State's presence in Iraq.

State and DOD Did Not Comply with Requirements for Use and Management of Assisted Acquisitions

In deciding to rely on DOD for 20 assisted acquisitions, State did not always comply with requirements for determining whether an assisted acquisition was the best procurement approach. For 12 of the assisted acquisitions, we found that determinations were not consistent with FAR and OMB requirements in terms of the extent to which certain factors were considered. For example, in deciding to use DOD's LOGCAP contract in Iraq, State did not assess cost-effectiveness. We also found that State and DOD did not prepare and sign interagency agreements for 13 of the 20 assisted acquisitions that contained certain factors designed to ensure strong management. For example, State and DOD did not identify roles and responsibilities as part of an interagency acquisition agreement prior to solicitation of the LOGCAP task order in January 2011. The State First policy for making and implementing decisions regarding interagency acquisitions has not been updated since 2008 to reflect current OMB guidance and FAR requirements for determinations of best procurement approach or interagency acquisition agreements. Furthermore, the Economy Act—which the departments cited as their authority for interagency acquisitions—requires that State reimburse DOD based on the actual costs of awarding and managing interagency acquisitions. In April 2012, the Army's Rock Island Contracting Center began tracking the staff-hours dedicated to assisted acquisitions supporting State in Iraq and Afghanistan and expects to submit the associated costs to State for payment. However, the departments have unresolved positions over whether State should reimburse DOD for the costs DOD incurred prior to January 2012. These positions could have been resolved if the departments had prepared and signed the required interagency acquisition agreements. The lack of compliance with guidance and regulation has implications for State's ability to make sound acquisition decisions. Specifically, State lacks the insight needed to assess alternative acquisition approaches and has not provided evidence of taking key acquisition planning steps. The expiration of key contracts supporting its presence in Iraq and changes to the U.S. presence in

State Did Not Comply with Requirements for Determining Best Procurement Approach

Afghanistan over the next 18 months compresses the time available for State to gain insights, plan, and make sound decisions about whether to continue to rely on interagency acquisitions or independently acquire critical goods and services.

The OMB guidance issued in 2008 and the FAR provisions regarding interagency acquisitions require agencies to make a determination that the use of an interagency acquisition represents the best procurement approach. In making this determination, the requesting agency—in this case, State—is to consider certain factors prior to requesting that a servicing agency—in this case, DOD—conduct an acquisition on its behalf. State officials told us they regard the justifications contained in the approved "waiver packets" prepared under the State First policy to be sufficient to meet FAR and OMB requirements.[33] However, the State First policy has not been updated since the issuance of OMB's 2008 guidance on improving the use of interagency acquisitions or the 2010 amendment to the FAR requiring a determination of best procurement approach.[34] These differences have implications for assisted interagency acquisitions, such as those we reviewed. OMB's guidance is intended to help agencies make sound business decisions to support the use of interagency acquisitions, and the purpose of the amendment to the FAR provisions on interagency acquisitions is to prevent abuse of interagency contracts by requiring a best procurement approach determination. The State First policy is silent with respect to how requesting bureaus wanting to enter into an interagency acquisition should make and document a determination of best procurement approach, putting the agency at risk

---

[33]In response to GAO requests for documentation of compliance with FAR and OMB requirements for a determination of best procurement approach for the assisted acquisitions within the scope of our review, State provided "waiver packets" prepared under its State First policy. Waiver packets provided included one or more of the following: waiver, internal memo, Economy Act determination and findings, Military Interdepartmental Purchase Request(s), and /or State standard form 1921 for award or modification of an interagency acquisition agreement. For our analysis of compliance with the requirement for a determination of best procurement approach, we reviewed waivers and internal memos because the other documents included in the waiver packets go to requirements other than the determination of best procurement approach. Under the State First policy, the waiver must contain certain information such as a description of the requirement, duration of the requirement, estimated value, and reason that using another agency for the acquisition is in the best interest of State.

[34]An interim rule was issued on December 13, 2010 and the final rule was issued on January 3, 2012. 75 Fed. Reg. 77,733, 77, 735; 77 Fed. Reg. 183.

for moving forward with an interagency acquisition that is not a sound business decision.

We found that for 12 of the 20 assisted acquisitions we reviewed, determinations of best procurement approach—documented through the State First waiver packets—were not made in accordance with the FAR and OMB requirements. In one case, a determination of best procurement approach was not made at all. In September 2010, State's mission in Afghanistan requested to receive dining facility services through DOD's LOGCAP contract. State's AQM and OPE did not approve a State First waiver or make any other determination of best procurement approach for this interagency acquisition. In the case of LOGCAP Iraq, the Near Eastern Affairs bureau's requirements for services under LOGCAP were not approved through a State First waiver before DOD proceeded with that interagency acquisition and State transferred funds to DOD.[35] Further, as shown in table 3, State did not always consider, as required, its full scope of requirements or cost-effectiveness when making a determination of best procurement approach.

Table 3: Summary of Noncompliance with OMB and FAR Requirements for Determination of Best Procurement Approach for 12 Assisted Acquisitions

Contract, task order, or modification	Considered full scope of requirements?	Considered cost-effectiveness?
LOGCAP (Afghanistan)[a]	○	○
LOGCAP (Iraq)	○	○
Sense and Warn Installation	●	○
Sense and Warn Operations	●	○
FIRST Maintenance	●	○
Food	○	●
Fuel (6 contracts)	○	●

Legend: ● Yes

○ No

Source: GAO analysis of State and DOD documents.

[a]No determination of best procurement approach was made.

---

[35]State prepared two waivers in support of its task order under LOGCAP Iraq. One waiver was for the Bureau of Diplomatic Security's requirements, which was approved in July 2011. The second waiver was for the Bureau of Near Eastern Affairs' requirements, which has not been approved and, according to AQM and Near Eastern Affairs officials, remains in draft form.

In the April and September 2010 letters from State to DOD requesting that DOD acquire goods and services on State's behalf and in the subsequent coordination activities between the departments, there was extensive discussion of some of the factors agencies are to consider when making a best procurement approach determination under the FAR requirements and OMB guidance. For example, State's request letters documented an urgent need that could be filled using DOD's contracts, and State indicated it had been satisfied with DOD's acquisition of the services as an existing customer. While these are among the factors agencies are to consider when making their determinations, subsequent events revealed that State did not have a full understanding of other factors, such as how its requirements would be met, when it decided to pursue interagency acquisitions with DOD.

This lack of full understanding can be illustrated by State's experience working with DOD to acquire basic support goods and services to support its mission in Iraq. In State's April 2010 letter to DOD requesting continued use of LOGCAP for basic services and use of associated food and fuel supply contracts, State highlighted how those contracts would meet its requirements. However, it appears that State did not have a full understanding of the scope of services and limitations of the contracts when it made its request. For example, under the terms of DLA's food contract, consistent with regulations regarding supply, certain goods cannot be acquired from the local economy.[36] According to State and DOD officials, State subsequently became aware of this limitation when it sought to have DOD modify the contract so that it could procure goods locally. In addition, by requesting to use the LOGCAP contract, State unknowingly took on additional security requirements because the contract requires that contractor personnel travel with a security escort. DOD had previously arranged for this security, but with DOD's withdrawal from Iraq, State had to make other security arrangements. According to State and DOD officials, including those in Iraq, after unsuccessful efforts to modify or eliminate security requirements from the contract, State requested that DOD award a task order under its existing SSS-I contract.

---

[36]Under the Javits-Wagner-O'Day Act, the Committee for Purchase from People Who Are Blind or Severely Disabled, that implements the AbilityOne program, maintains a procurement list of all supplies and services required to be purchased from AbilityOne participating nonprofit organizations. Supply distribution facilities in DLA are required to obtain supplies on the procurement list from the central nonprofit organization identified or its designated AbilityOne participating nonprofit organization. 41 U.S.C. § 8503-04; FAR § 8.705-1.

Furthermore, State officials did not believe it was necessary to provide security for convoys of food and fuel. However, State ultimately decided to do so based on discussions with DOD and coordination with supplier companies. In requesting and justifying its use of LOGCAP and DLA supply contracts, State did not acknowledge these additional requirements or their implications as part of its decision to rely on DOD.

Similarly, we found that State First waiver packets and other documentation did not fully implement the FAR's requirement that cost-effectiveness be considered in making the determination of best procurement approach. For example, neither the State First waiver prepared for use of DOD's contract for sustainment of equipment nor the waiver prepared for use of DOD's Sense and Warn capability assessed cost-effectiveness. Further, there is evidence that State's decision to rely on DOD's LOGCAP contract in Iraq did not consider cost-effectiveness. In State's April 2010 request to use LOGCAP, the justification does not refer to cost-effectiveness. A subsequent September 2010 DOD memorandum authorizing DOD components' implementation of that request concluded, "DOD cannot provide the [requested] support at a lower cost or more quickly than could State contracting independently." DOD's assessment of the costs also noted that "the amounts requested by State are likely to be significantly less than the actual cost of the support," which were estimated at the time to be at least $63 million annually. Indeed, over the 15 months following State's initial request to use LOGCAP, requirements for services changed and associated costs rose to an estimated $219 million for 2012 at the time DOD awarded State's LOGCAP task order. However, the State First waiver submitted by the Bureau of Diplomatic Security in July 2011 stated, in the cost-benefit analysis section, that market research or other comparison methods were not used because of the urgency of the requirement. Although State's decision to request LOGCAP to sustain critical goods and services to avoid mission failure may have been reasonable under the circumstances, the absence of any subsequent effort to assess cost-effectiveness is not only contrary to acquisition regulation but also limits the department's understanding of expected resource needs, ability to plan and budget for future costs, and evaluate other options in the future for meeting this requirement.

State and DOD Did Not Fully Meet Requirements for Assisted Interagency Acquisition Agreements

Although State and DOD coordinated to identify State's acquisition needs for Iraq and made a series of decisions on what DOD would provide, how the departments documented and implemented these decisions was in some cases inconsistent with the FAR and OMB guidance intended to ensure effective management of interagency acquisitions. Specifically, the regulation and guidance require agencies to enter into written agreements to govern assisted interagency acquisitions. For 13 of the 20 assisted acquisitions we reviewed, State and DOD either did not prepare an agreement, did not both sign the agreement, or the agreement did not contain required elements designed to ensure effective management.

Formal interagency acquisition agreements establishing roles and responsibilities help ensure strong management. We previously reported that a lack of clear definitions of roles and responsibilities is a significant risk with interagency acquisitions.[37] To help mitigate that risk, the FAR and OMB's 2008 guidance on strengthening the management of interagency acquisitions direct agencies to have in place prior to solicitation of a contract or task order a written interagency acquisition agreement that, among other things:[38]

- defines roles and responsibilities for contract management,
- describes goods or services covered in order to demonstrate a bona fide need,
- includes funding information from both the requesting and servicing agency to ensure the proper transfer and obligation of funds, and
- identifies unique terms and conditions that apply for the requesting agency.

Under the State First policy, once AQM and OPE approve a bureau's State First waiver, AQM is required to work with the bureau to prepare an interagency acquisition agreement with the servicing agency. The agreement may be prepared on a State standard form and must contain (1) a description of the supplies or services required, (2) delivery requirements, (3) a funds citation, (4) a payment provision, and

---

[37]GAO, *High-Risk Series: An Update*, GAO 11-278 (Washington, D.C.: February 2011).

[38]FAR § 17.502-1(b)(1) and OMB, Office of the Federal Procurement Policy, *Improving the Management and Use of Interagency Acquisitions* (Washington, D.C.: June 6, 2008). The OMB guidance provides that part A of an interagency agreement, which sets out the general terms and conditions, may cover multiple assisted acquisitions.

(5) acquisition authority as may be appropriate. The State First policy generally aligns with the FAR provisions regarding interagency acquisitions under the Economy Act in effect prior to the 2010 amendment to FAR. However, the State First policy has not been updated since the issuance of OMB's 2008 guidance on improving the management of interagency acquisitions by ensuring interagency agreements for assisted acquisitions contain certain elements or the FAR amendment requiring a written agreement on responsibility for management and administration for assisted acquisitions. Under State's policy, an interagency agreement may be documented on a standard one-page form. Completion of this form does not meet the requirements for a written interagency agreement delineated in the FAR and OMB guidance because the form does not require details such as roles and responsibilities for contract administration and management. Among other things, identifying roles and responsibilities is critical to ensuring effective management of an interagency acquisition.

DOD policy also mandates the use of interagency acquisition agreements. The Director, Defense Procurement and Acquisition Policy, issued a memorandum in October 2008 to implement OMB's 2008 guidance, and we found it to be consistent with that guidance and current FAR provisions. In addition, for all interagency acquisitions over $500,000—which includes all of the interagency acquisitions we reviewed—DOD's memorandum directs that interagency acquisition agreements contain the elements or follow the model in the interagency acquisition agreement template provided in OMB's guidance.

Although written interagency acquisition agreements were required for all 20 of the assisted acquisitions we reviewed, State and DOD did not consistently prepare them in accordance with acquisition regulation and guidance, as shown in table 4.

Table 4: Status of Interagency Agreements for 20 Assisted Acquisitions

Contract, task order, or modification	Agreement prepared	Signed by both departments
Food	●	●
Fuel (6 contracts)	●	●
LOGCAP (Iraq)	◉	○
SSS-I (for LOGCAP)	◉	○
SSS-I (for food and fuel)	◉	○
LOGCAP (Afghanistan)	○	○
TWISS (5 task orders)	○	○
Sense and Warn Installation	○	○
Sense and Warn Operations	○	○
FIRST Maintenance	○	○
Vetting	○	○

Legend: ● Yes

○ No

◉ Did not meet one or more requirements

Source: GAO analysis of State and DOD documents

Seven of the 20 acquisitions were covered by an interagency acquisition agreement between State and DLA that contained the required elements, such as roles and responsibilities, designed to ensure effective management of the acquisition. Of the remaining 13, interagency acquisition agreements were prepared for 3, but these agreements were not signed by both departments prior to solicitation and did not contain roles and responsibilities or other elements. For example, State officials prepared standard one-page Department of State forms for the LOGCAP task order and two SSS-I task orders, but DOD officials did not sign the forms. Further, these forms did not specify State's requirements for the acquisition or the respective roles and responsibilities for State and DOD. The other 10 assisted acquisitions were not covered by any interagency acquisition agreement, which contributed to confusion and limited effective management of the acquisitions.[39]

According to State and DOD officials, in lieu of formal interagency acquisition agreements, DOD's acquisition assistance was implemented at the lowest possible organizational level. State and DOD officials identified the Executive Steering Group, which was established in September 2010, as well as the associated Embassy Support and Enduring Base Transition Board, as the primary mechanisms of coordinating and implementing DOD's acquisition support. The Executive Steering Group meets on at least a bi-weekly basis. According to Executive Steering Group leadership, it does not have any decision-making authority but rather helps identify issues and relevant officials or organizations that might address them and tracks the progress of the issues to resolution. The departments' Principal Under Secretary of Defense for Acquisition, Technology, and Logistics and Under Secretary of State for Management provide guidance and make decisions pertaining to issues raised in the group on an as-needed basis. Though a draft charter for the group was prepared, officials noted a determination was made not to finalize it, as they believed the goodwill between the departments was sufficient to resolve any disagreements.

While the Executive Steering Group facilitated discussion and identified acquisition issues, the group's activities did not replace the departments' responsibilities under the FAR and OMB guidance for formalizing written interagency acquisition agreements. Executive Steering Group members from both departments informed us that they did not consider State's reliance on DOD to acquire critical goods and services in these instances as constituting assisted acquisitions that required interagency agreements, even though group membership included State acquisition officials and DOD acquisition and financial management officials. For example, senior State and DOD officials told us that the departments did not enter into written interagency acquisition agreements for LOGCAP or SSS-I because of their understanding that the Military Interdepartmental

---

[39]With respect to State's use of LOGCAP in Afghanistan, the U.S. Forces-Afghanistan and the U.S. mission in Afghanistan entered into a memorandum of agreement in August 2009 for the support of personnel acting under the authority of the chief of mission to implement the U.S. strategy in Afghanistan. The agreement is an umbrella agreement intended to provide a baseline direction for support responsibilities, rather than an interagency acquisition agreement for a specific interagency acquisition.

Purchase Requests submitted by State were sufficient to facilitate agreement and associated reimbursement.[40] However, Diplomatic Security officials responsible for preparing waivers and processing payment for the assisted acquisitions acknowledged that interagency acquisition agreements were required. They stated that AQM did not pursue agreements due to the urgency of the needs and the limited time for DOD to execute contract actions on State's behalf. Standard one-page interagency agreement forms were prepared for both LOGCAP and SSS-I, indicating recognition at some level within AQM that these acquisitions were interagency acquisitions. These one-page forms, however, did not meet FAR requirements and OMB guidance, such as specifying the departments' respective roles and responsibilities.

By not having formalized agreements in place prior to solicitation, State and DOD experienced significant expectation gaps about roles and responsibilities. These gaps delayed establishment of contract oversight responsibility and contractor performance standards. Although the departments eventually reached mutual understanding through discussions at the Executive Steering Group, the process was inefficient and the delays were avoidable. For example:

- A one-page interagency agreement form for the use of LOGCAP in Iraq was prepared by State in January 2011 but never signed by DOD. The form did not define the roles and responsibilities for acquisition activities between State and DOD, including contract oversight. Resulting disagreements between DOD and State regarding which department would provide CORs persisted for several months, leading to DCMA not entering into an agreement to support State without State first identifying its CORs and agreeing to train them to DOD standards. State eventually agreed to provide 18 full- and part-time oversight personnel, and DCMA provided 26 quality assurance representatives with specific subject matter expertise for overseeing the contractor, in support of the State personnel. Although that agreement was reached in February 2012, it was delayed over a year beyond solicitation of the LOGCAP task order as State and DCMA officials resolved issues related to the

---

[40]Although OMB's guidance identifies Military Interdepartmental Purchase Requests as one of the forms that can facilitate interagency transfers, it also directs that these requests incorporate by reference or attachment the terms and conditions of an overarching interagency acquisition agreement, which State did not do for these acquisitions.

oversight roles and responsibilities, as well as the associated payment for DCMA's services.

- State prepared a one-page interagency agreement form covering two SSS-I task orders DOD awarded on State's behalf, which DOD did not sign. The form did not identify unique terms and conditions that applied to State, as required by the FAR and OMB guidance, which in this case pertained to security contracts. Given the transition in responsibility from DOD to State for the mission in Iraq, DOD contracting officials raised concerns throughout the summer of 2011 over the continued use of DOD security contractor performance standards, such as rules of engagement. State ultimately decided to use its own performance standards, but the delay in reaching agreement regarding security standards delayed task order award by 2 months.

In contrast, DCAA and DCMA entered into agreements with State, covering their specific roles in administration, oversight, and audits across the 20 assisted acquisitions. DCAA and DCMA provide support across multiple organizations both within and outside DOD and regularly use agreements to formalize that support. Since 1983, State has received DCAA's contract audit services under an agreement generally renewed annually. In addition, since 2003, DCAA's Iraq Branch Office has been supporting both DOD's and State's acquisitions in Iraq; the agreement was modified in December 2011 to support State's requirements following DOD's departure. In February 2012, State entered into a memorandum of agreement with DCMA for contract administration support for the contracts awarded on behalf of State with performance in Iraq, including LOGCAP. The agreements with DCAA and DCMA pertain to only those agencies' specific activities with respect to the covered acquisitions. As such, these agreements do not fulfill OMB and FAR requirements for interagency acquisition agreements as they do not cover other activities and responsible parties, such as performing contract award and administration on State's behalf.

Payment for Certain Costs Associated with Assisted Interagency Acquisitions Remain Unresolved

The actual costs to a servicing agency in an Economy Act assisted interagency acquisition generally include both the costs of the contracted goods or services, as well as the costs associated with the servicing agency's commitment of personnel and other resources to plan and execute the contract action on the requesting agency's behalf. For example, beginning with State's requests in 2010 for DOD's assistance under the Economy Act, DOD committed personnel and other resources to plan and execute the contract actions on State's behalf. State provided payments to DOD for the costs of the contracted goods and services for the 20 assisted interagency acquisitions in our review. For some of these acquisitions, however, State has not yet paid DOD for other direct or indirect costs of providing goods and services. After we raised questions regarding State's payment for actual costs, DOD legal officials have taken the position that State should pay DOD for these costs and are now in the process of determining the amount State should pay going back to 2010. In contrast, State legal officials have taken the position that State is prohibited from paying DOD for the costs associated with awarding and supporting the interagency acquisitions prior to 2012. These positions are unresolved. Had the departments formalized interagency acquisition agreements in accordance with the FAR and OMB guidance, these issues could have been resolved prior to moving forward with these acquisitions. Furthermore, unresolved positions on the terms and extent of State's payment to DOD place the departments at risk of non-compliance with fiscal law.[41]

Departments Have Not Resolved Whether State Is Required to Pay DOD for Certain Costs Prior to 2012

The Economy Act was the authority used for the interagency acquisitions in our review. For interagency acquisitions under the authority of the Economy Act, the requesting agency is required to pay the servicing agency on the basis of the actual cost of entering into and administering the contract on the requesting agency's behalf.[42] In determining actual costs, agencies must avoid the unauthorized augmentation of their appropriations, as charging too much would augment the servicing agency's appropriations, while charging too little would augment the requesting agency's appropriations. The Economy Act requires that the actual costs include all direct costs attributable to the performance of a service or furnishing of materials, regardless of whether the servicing

---

[41]Fiscal law provides that an agency generally must use its appropriated funds for the purposes for which the appropriations were made. 31 U.S.C. § 1301(a). In addition, an agency receiving goods or services funded by another agency's appropriations must reimburse the servicing agency to avoid improperly augmenting the requesting agency's appropriations. Furthermore, payments received by the servicing agency for goods or services provided, without other statutory authority, must be deposited into the Treasury as miscellaneous receipts. 31 U.S.C. § 3302(b).

[42]31 U.S.C. § 1535(b); FAR § 17.502-2(d)(4). Although precise calculations of actual costs are not required, the amount to be paid should result from a bona fide attempt to determine actual cost and should reasonably approximate actual cost. For a discussion of payment requirements under the Economy Act, see GAO, *Principles of Federal Appropriations Law*, 3rd ed. Vol. 3, ch. 12.B.1. GAO-08-978SP (Washington, D.C.: September 2008).

agency's expenditures were thereby increased.[43] Direct costs include salaries for employees doing the work.[44] Actual cost also includes certain indirect costs (overhead) proportionately allocable to the transaction, such as administrative overhead applicable to supervision.[45]

Legal officials from both departments informed us that State paid the Army's Rock Island Contracting Center for the costs of the LOGCAP, SSS-I, vetting, and FIRST maintenance contracted services. However, these officials informed us that State has not paid for the Center's costs associated with the personnel working on these acquisitions on State's behalf or other indirect overhead costs. The departments have not resolved their positions with respect to whether State should pay DOD for these costs going back to 2010, when coordination activities began for these interagency acquisitions. DOD legal officials told us they had determined that the Economy Act requires State to pay DOD for the costs associated with award and management of the task orders and contract modification on State's behalf, as these costs are part of the interagency acquisitions' actual costs. In response to our questions regarding State's payment for these costs, the Army's Rock Island Contracting Center established a process in April 2012 to document time expended in support of State acquisitions going forward and has also identified those personnel who have been providing support to State. For example, Center officials estimated that approximately 12 full-time equivalent staff had been supporting State's LOGCAP task order alone since the summer of 2010, when acquisition planning activities began. The Center has not yet finalized its calculation of the hours and associated costs but has indicated that upon finalization it will submit this information to State for payment.

State legal officials agreed that the department is required, in accordance with the Economy Act, to pay DOD on the basis of actual costs—to

---

[43]Otherwise, the servicing agency would be penalized to the extent that its funds are used to finance the cost of performing another agency's work, while the requesting agency's appropriations are augmented to the extent that they now may be used for some other purpose. 57 Comp. Gen. 674, 682.

[44]12 Comp. Gen. 442.

[45]Specifically, indirect costs which are funded out of currently available appropriations and bear a significant relationship to the service or work performed or the materials furnished are recoverable in an Economy Act transaction the same as direct costs. 56 Comp. Gen. 275.

GAO-12-750 Iraq and Afghanistan

include costs associated with contract award and management—but believe this applies only to costs incurred after December 31, 2011. State legal officials informed us that State is prohibited from paying DOD for support provided prior to December 31, 2011, because doing so would improperly augment DOD's appropriations. State legal officials point to language in National Security Presidential Directive 36 directing departments to provide support to U.S. activities in Iraq on a non-reimbursable basis and stating that the Director of OMB shall ensure budget submissions shall request funding necessary to support the U.S. mission in Iraq. State legal officials maintain that DOD was directed to include support costs—such as the cost of personnel who awarded and administer task orders on State's behalf and other indirect overhead costs—in its budget requests so DOD would receive adequate appropriations for these purposes. These officials further maintain that providing payment to DOD for the same costs would augment DOD's appropriations. State and DOD's positions regarding payment requirements have not yet been resolved, which leaves the departments vulnerable to non-compliance with fiscal law.

Departments Missed Opportunities to Clarify and Resolve Payment Terms

The departments' positions with respect to payment for certain costs associated with the assisted interagency acquisitions we reviewed should have been resolved prior to moving forward with the acquisitions through formalizing agreements between them. In the September 2010 meeting establishing the Executive Steering Group, a draft charter was presented to provide organization and operating guidance for DOD to transfer equipment and develop sourcing solutions for State requirements. This draft charter notes that the Office of the Secretary of Defense, Comptroller will advise the group to ensure statutory compliance with the Economy Act, with general counsel to assist. This charter was never finalized, and thus, the departments' leadership missed an opportunity to formalize the role of the Comptroller, who could have clarified the terms of payment associated with DOD's support. Senior State and DOD officials who participated in the Executive Steering Group told us they understood there to be an agreement in principle for State to pay DOD for actual costs. However, they could not provide evidence that DOD was being paid for any costs other than the costs of the contracted goods and services.

Further, had the departments executed interagency acquisition agreements containing the elements enumerated in the FAR and OMB guidance, the departments' positions regarding payment would have been aligned. Under OMB guidance, an interagency acquisition agreement should contain specific terms for payment to ensure agreement on these terms between the agencies.[46] Without these agreements, terms for payment were unclear, resulting in the departments' positions being unresolved for these five interagency acquisitions. For example, the September 2010 memorandum signed by the Deputy Secretary of Defense authorized the provision of basic life support to State through the Army's LOGCAP contract on a reimbursable basis; however, Army officials indicated that there was an open question as to whether associated support costs were to be reimbursed. Had the departments executed an interagency acquisition agreement prior to issuance of the solicitation for the LOGCAP task order supporting State, as required under the FAR, the departments would have established a mutual understanding with respect to reimbursable costs. In contrast, the annual renewals to the memorandum of agreement that State has in place with DCAA provide for State to reimburse DCAA for the services provided to State in 2011 and 2012 under the Economy Act. The memorandum of agreement that State has with DCMA provides for the reimbursement of services in fiscal year 2012 under the Economy Act.

State Lacks Insight to Assess Alternative Approaches for Future Acquisitions

In sustaining its presence in Iraq and Afghanistan, State faces important decisions for how to acquire critical goods and services as it goes forward. To be consistent with FAR requirements, State's decision to continue relying on DOD for the acquisition of critical goods and services should entail assessing procurement approaches—such as independently acquiring the goods and services—to determine the best approach.[47] However, State has had limited insight into the acquisition process for the basic support and security services provided under DOD contracts. Further, while the Rock Island Contracting Center has recently begun tracking the hours its personnel spend supporting assisted acquisitions on State's behalf, DOD has not yet reported the associated costs to State. State's ability to assess approaches and make informed decisions about whether to continue relying on DOD's contracts through interagency acquisitions is hindered until State can fully evaluate the actual costs of DOD's acquisition support.

---

[46]OMB's guidance provides that an interagency agreement must include financial information that is required to authorize the transfer and obligation of funds for both the acquisition and the assistance provided by the servicing agency in connection with the acquisition.

[47]FAR § 17.502-1(a)(1).

To help State identify available procurement alternatives to meet its continuing requirements in Iraq, State and DOD established a Transition Phase II Working Group in early 2012. However, the amount of time available for State to make and implement acquisition decisions is shrinking as key contracts are set to expire over the next 18 months. If State is to independently acquire needed fuel, food, and basic support services, it would need to perform acquisition planning and market research under the FAR, as soon as the need is identified.[48] State officials have taken some steps to determine whether independently acquiring fuel and food may be a cost-effective procurement alternative to DOD-awarded contracts. State officials informed us of plans to award their own fuel contract to replace DOD's contract that expires in September 2012. Additionally, in January 2012, State awarded a contract for market research on local sources of food, considering factors such as quality assurance standards, reliability, and pricing. However, State's current efforts to assess procurement approaches for basic support services may not be sufficient to determine whether LOGCAP or a State-awarded contract is the best approach. According to DOD acquisition officials, State would need at least 11 to 12 months of acquisition planning to independently acquire basic support services given their complexity. State officials have not provided evidence that they are taking key acquisition planning steps, such as estimating the costs of directly acquiring the services or drafting an acquisition plan to identify alternatives. Even though DOD's LOGCAP contract expires in December 2013, State's April 2010 request for LOGCAP anticipated using it beyond 2013 and potentially until 2015. In May 2012 State acquisition officials informed us of their intent to transition from LOGCAP to State contracts by October 2013; however, they provided no documentation of this acquisition planning. With respect to security capabilities, DOD has an expectation that State will assume contract oversight and sustainment support operations for the FIRST maintenance contract in September 2012, leaving State only months to identify a procurement alternative and make a decision. Not only does State have limited time to identify and pursue an alternative, but State officials have also acknowledged that

---

[48]FAR § 7.102. FAR Part 10 describes the policies and procedures for conducting market research to determine the most suitable approach to acquiring, distributing, and supporting supplies and services. GAO has also reported on important elements of successful acquisition planning, such as developing requirements, cost estimating, incorporating lessons learned, and allowing sufficient time to conduct acquisition planning. See GAO, *Acquisition Planning: Opportunities to Build Strong Foundations for Better Services Contracts*, GAO-11-672 (Washington, D.C.: Aug. 9, 2011).

DOD's expertise better positions it to acquire services related to military capabilities, such as Sense and Warn.

For Afghanistan, as the departments prepare to realign their presence to meet national security policy objectives, State's current planning efforts similarly may not be sufficient to identify procurement alternatives and determine a best procurement approach. State has incorporated some knowledge gained through acquiring critical goods and services in Iraq to inform planning for Afghanistan. For example, State and DOD officials told us they established an Executive Steering Group for Afghanistan modeled on the group for Iraq. In addition, State established the Management Transition Office in June 2011 to help with transition planning in Afghanistan for a post-2014 presence. As part of this office, a Logistics Support and Services Working Group is expected to determine detailed requirements for support areas such as fuel and life support. The group will also take on specific tasks, such as developing food service contract alternatives that eliminate reliance on DOD contracts. The Executive Steering Group and State's working group responsibilities represent a key acquisition-planning step—developing requirements. However, State has not yet provided evidence that it has taken steps to address other key elements of acquisition planning, such as estimating the costs of either independently acquiring the goods and services or relying on DOD for support. In addition, the description of the working group's membership and activities do not include State's AQM. As a result, State is not formally including key contracting staff responsible for determining the best procurement approach as called for in the FAR and OMB guidance.

Conclusions

The Departments of Defense and State faced many challenges in completing the transition from a U.S. military to a civilian-led presence in Iraq. In particular, planning for the State-led presence in Iraq while negotiating for a potential follow-on military force of an unknown size placed State and DOD in an uncertain position to make decisions on how best to arrange for medical, security, and basic support services and associated goods critical to maintaining State's mission. At the same time, both departments were also engaged in carrying out their respective missions in Afghanistan. In assisting State with acquisitions to support its presence in both Iraq and Afghanistan, DOD leveraged its acquisition capacity and expertise to award and manage contracts to meet complex requirements in conflict environments. State and DOD officials extensively collaborated and took extraordinary measures in some cases to ensure that the delivery of critical contracted goods and services were not interrupted to prevent mission failure. However, the way State made decisions to request and rely on DOD's acquisition assistance and how the two departments went about implementing those decisions did not comply with regulation and guidance. In particular, the departments missed opportunities to ensure that sound decisions were made after fully considering cost effectiveness and requirements and that agreements for the effective management and sufficient oversight of those acquisitions were in place. These missed opportunities can be attributed, in part, to an outdated State First policy that does not reflect current regulation and guidance intended to improve the management of interagency acquisitions, as well as efforts by officials under challenging circumstances to manage these acquisitions through more informal means.

Because the departments did not follow relevant guidance and regulation in implementing the interagency acquisitions we reviewed, DOD and State now have unresolved positions regarding payment for DOD's assistance. Both departments cited the authority of the Economy Act as the mechanism enabling DOD's assistance, which requires that State pay DOD for certain costs incurred in awarding and managing the assisted acquisitions on State's behalf. However, the departments' positions regarding whether State should reimburse DOD for task order award and contract management activities in 2010 and 2011 supporting State's current presence in Iraq are unresolved. Without resolution of these positions, the departments are at risk of not being in compliance with fiscal law.

How State and DOD made and implemented decisions regarding the interagency acquisitions supporting State's presence in Iraq and Afghanistan also has implications for future acquisitions. State is not well positioned to make informed decisions as to whether it should continue to rely on DOD or independently pursue acquiring critical goods and services to maintain its presence in Iraq and Afghanistan. It is important for State to determine whether and to what extent interagency acquisitions are the appropriate means not only to support its evolving presence in Iraq and Afghanistan but also to support the development of the expeditionary capacity to address any future conflicts and crises around the world called for by State's Quadrennial Diplomacy and Development Review. Such determinations are to be informed by the consideration of various factors as to whether interagency acquisitions are the best procurement approach to fulfill a specific need. Limitations in State's planning for future basic support services currently provided under DOD's LOGCAP contract increases the risk of repeating the same sequence of events that led State to urgently request DOD's acquisition assistance in April 2010. The Army's Rock Island Contracting Center is now tracking personnel hours expended in the award and management of assisted acquisitions on State's behalf. Use of such information, if provided in time, can better inform State's evaluation of procurement approaches for basic support goods and services and security services.

For State to independently contract for any of the goods and services currently provided through DOD contracts to support its presence in Iraq and Afghanistan, time is short to plan for how it will proceed after current assisted acquisitions end. This planning requires a robust understanding of both the support State currently relies on DOD to provide and the limitations of State's own acquisition capacity—including contracting and subject matter expertise. Yet State has not taken a number of steps to ensure that its acquisition workforce can support future contracting efforts in Iraq, Afghanistan, or similar environments, including assessing whether its working capital fund is a sufficient mechanism to meet surge requirements; it has the proper skill and government/contractor mix in its acquisition workforce; and it has sufficient numbers of qualified oversight personnel. Both State and DOD currently have an opportunity to assess and reach agreement on whether continued reliance is appropriate or whether State should develop its own capacity. It is imperative that the departments do so now before the lessons from recent experiences are lost. Without taking steps to inform those assessments that consider the costs and time to build requisite expertise, State risks continued reliance on DOD assisted acquisitions by default rather than through sound business decisions.

Recommendations for Executive Action

To ensure that current and future assisted interagency acquisitions in support of State's missions in Iraq and Afghanistan are consistent with regulatory requirements and guidance designed to improve the management and use of such acquisitions, we recommend that the Secretary of State and Secretary of Defense undertake a comprehensive review of all existing and proposed assisted interagency acquisitions in support of State's missions in Iraq and Afghanistan to identify and implement corrective measures to bring the acquisitions into compliance and to strengthen management. Specifically, this should entail

- the Department of State assessing the cost effectiveness and full range of requirements, which can be used to inform future best procurement approach determinations,

- the Departments of State and Defense preparing and signing interagency acquisition agreements that address the elements established in the FAR and OMB guidance, such as roles and responsibilities for contract management and oversight, and
- the Department of State planning for sufficient personnel to perform contract oversight.

To better inform future decisions regarding the use of assisted interagency acquisitions and to better manage and more consistently implement their use, we recommend that the Secretary of State revise the State First policy to fully align with current FAR and OMB requirements regarding interagency acquisitions.

To ensure proper payment between the departments in accordance with fiscal law, we recommend that the Secretary of Defense and the Secretary of State work to jointly resolve their positions with respect to payment for DOD's direct and indirect costs of providing the goods and services to State under the interagency acquisitions we reviewed and take appropriate action according to their resolution.

To ensure that its acquisition workforce has sufficient capacity to meet the need for acquiring critical goods and services for unique and complex environments like Iraq and Afghanistan that the Department of State may choose to independently acquire, we recommend that Secretary of State

- identify, in consultation with DOD, areas of contracting and subject matter expertise needed, along with the number of personnel needed, to acquire goods and services in such environments; assess the extent to which the current acquisition workforce meets those needs; and based on the results of that assessment, incorporate efforts to build that expertise and personnel numbers into State's acquisition workforce planning and
- based on those identified needs and resulting workforce planning, assess whether the acquisition workforce working capital fund as it currently operates is a sufficient mechanism to surge State's acquisition workforce capacity with the appropriate personnel, both in terms of expertise and numbers, and mix of government and contractor personnel to support State's missions in such environments and evaluate whether changes to the fund or other actions are needed.

Agency Comments

We provided a draft of this report to DOD and State for their review and comment. Both DOD and State concurred with our recommendations in their written comments, which are reproduced in appendix I and appendix II respectively. In concurring with our recommendations, State noted it is revising its policies to align with current FAR and OMB requirements and it has engaged with DOD to ensure proper payment between the departments in accordance with fiscal law. State also indicated an expectation to use our assessment and a recently initiated State Office of Inspector General review to guide its efforts to address our recommendation regarding its acquisition workforce. DOD also provided a technical comment that was incorporated into the final report.

We are sending copies of this report to interested congressional committees, the Secretary of State, and the Secretary of Defense. In addition, the report will be available at no charge on GAO's website at http://www.gao.gov.

If you or your staff have questions about this report, please contact me at (202) 512-4841 or huttonj@gao.gov. Contact points for our Offices of Congressional Relations and Public Affairs may be found on the last page of this report. GAO staff who made major contributions to this report are listed in appendix III.

John P. Hutton
Director
Acquisition and Sourcing Management

List of Committees

The Honorable Carl Levin
Chairman
The Honorable John McCain
Ranking Member
Committee on Armed Services
United States Senate

The Honorable John Kerry
Chairman
The Honorable Richard G. Lugar
Ranking Member
Committee on Foreign Relations
United States Senate

The Honorable Joseph I. Lieberman
Chairman
The Honorable Susan M. Collins
Ranking Member
Committee on Homeland Security and Governmental Affairs
United States Senate

The Honorable Claire McCaskill
Chairman
The Honorable Rob Portman
Ranking Member
Ad Hoc Subcommittee on Contracting Oversight
Committee on Homeland Security and Governmental Affairs
United States Senate

The Honorable Howard P. "Buck" McKeon
Chairman
The Honorable Adam Smith
Ranking Member
Committee on Armed Services
House of Representatives

The Honorable Ileana Ros-Lehtinen
Chairman
The Honorable Howard Berman
Ranking Member
Committee on Foreign Affairs
House of Representatives

The Honorable Darrell E. Issa
Chairman
The Honorable Elijah E. Cummings
Ranking Member
Committee on Oversight and Government Reform
House of Representatives

Appendix I: Comments from the Department of Defense

OFFICE OF THE UNDER SECRETARY OF DEFENSE
3000 DEFENSE PENTAGON
WASHINGTON, DC 20301-3000

ACQUISITION,
TECHNOLOGY
AND LOGISTICS

JUL 31 2012

Mr. John P. Hutton
Director, Acquisition and Sourcing Management
U.S. Government Accountability Office
441 G Street, N.W.
Washington, DC 20548

Dear Mr. Hutton:

This is the Department of Defense (DoD) response to the GAO Draft Report, GAO-12-750SU, "IRAQ AND AFGHANISTAN: State and DOD Should Ensure Interagency Acquisitions are Effectively Managed and Comply with Fiscal Law," dated June 27, 2012, (GAO Code 120976). Detailed comments on the report recommendations are enclosed. Technical comments were provided separately for your consideration.

Sincerely,

Richard Ginman
Director, Defense Procurement
and Acquisition Policy

Enclosure:
as stated

GAO Draft Report Dated JUNE 27, 2012
GAO-12-750SU (GAO CODE 120976)

"IRAQ AND AFGHANISTAN: STATE AND DOD SHOULD ENSURE INTERAGENCY
ACQUISITIONS ARE EFFECTIVELY MANAGED AND COMPLY WITH FISCAL
LAW"

DEPARTMENT OF DEFENSE COMMENTS
TO THE GAO RECOMMENDATIONS

RECOMMENDATION 1: The GAO recommends that the Secretary of State and Secretary of
Defense undertake a comprehensive review of all existing and proposed assisted interagency
acquisitions in support of State's missions in Iraq and Afghanistan to identify and implement
corrective measures to bring the acquisitions into compliance and to strengthen management.
Specifically this should entail the Departments of State and Defense preparing and signing
interagency acquisition agreements that address the elements established in the FAR and OMB
guidance, such as roles and responsibilities for contract management and oversight.

DoD RESPONSE: DoD concurs with this recommendation.

RECOMMENDATION 2: The GAO recommends that the Secretary of Defense and the
Secretary of State work to jointly resolve their positions with respect to payment for DOD's
direct and indirect costs of providing the goods and service to State under the interagency
acquisitions we reviewed, and take appropriate action according to their resolution.

DoD RESPONSE: DoD concurs with this recommendation.

Appendix II: Comments from the Department of State

United States Department of State

Comptroller
1969 Dyess Avenue
Charleston, SC 29405

Dr. Loren Yager
Managing Director
International Affairs and Trade
Government Accountability Office
441 G Street, N.W.
Washington, D.C. 20548-0001

JUL 2 5 2012

Dear Dr. Yager:

We appreciate the opportunity to review your draft report, "IRAQ AND AFGHANISTAN: State and DOD Should Ensure Interagency Acquisitions are Effectively Managed and Comply with Fiscal Law" GAO Job Code 120976.

The enclosed Department of State comments are provided for incorporation with this letter as an appendix to the final report.

If you have any questions concerning this response, please contact Renee Bemish, Special Assistant, Bureau of Administration at (202) 647-4461.

Sincerely,

James L. Millette

cc: GAO – John P. Hutton
A – Joyce A. Barr
State/OIG – Evelyn Klemstine

<u>**Department of State Comments on GAO Draft Report**</u>

<u>**DEPARTMENT OF STATE: Iraq and Afghanistan-
State and DOD Should Ensure Interagency Acquisitions are Effectively
Managed and Comply with Fiscal Law**</u>
(GAO-12-750SU, GAO Code 120976)

The Department of State appreciates the opportunity to comment on GAO's draft report on the management of State and DOD interagency acquisitions relating to unprecedented responsibilities in Iraq and Afghanistan.

<u>Recommendation:</u> To ensure that current and future assisted interagency acquisitions in support of State's missions in Iraq and Afghanistan are consistent with regulatory requirements and guidance designed to improve the management and use of such acquisitions, we recommend that the Secretary of State and Secretary of Defense undertake a comprehensive review of all existing and proposed assisted interagency acquisitions in support of State's missions in Iraq and Afghanistan to identify and implement corrective measures to bring the acquisitions into compliance and to strengthen management. Specifically, this should entail

- the Department of State assessing the cost effectiveness and full range of requirements, which can be used to inform future best procurement approach determinations,

- the Departments of State and Defense preparing and signing interagency acquisition agreements that address the elements established in the FAR and OMB guidance, such as roles and responsibilities for contract management and oversight, and

- the Department of State planning for sufficient personnel to perform contract oversight.

<u>Response:</u> The Department concurs with the recommendation to identify and implement corrective measures to bring all acquisitions into compliance and to strengthen contract management and oversight.

<u>Recommendation:</u> To better inform future decisions regarding the use of assisted interagency acquisition and to better manage and more consistently

2

implement their use, we recommend that the Secretary of State revise the State First policy to fully align with current FAR and OMB requirements regarding interagency acquisitions.

Response: The Department concurs and is revising Department policies to fully align with current FAR and OMB requirements.

Recommendation: To ensure proper payment between the departments in accordance with fiscal law, we recommend that the Secretary of Defense and the Secretary of State work to jointly resolve their positions with respect to payment for DOD's direct and indirect costs of providing the goods and services to State under the interagency acquisitions we reviewed, and take appropriate action according to their resolution.

Response: The Department concurs with the recommendation and has engaged DOD to resolve this issue.

Recommendation: To ensure that its acquisition workforce has sufficient capacity to meet the need for acquiring critical goods and services for unique and complex environments like Iraq and Afghanistan that the Department of State may choose to independently acquire, we recommend that Secretary of State

- identify, in consultation with DOD, areas of contracting and subject matter expertise needed, along with the number of personnel needed, to acquire goods and services in such environments; assess the extent to which the current acquisition workforce meets those needs; and based on the results of that assessment, incorporate efforts to build that expertise and personnel numbers into State's acquisition workforce planning; and

- based on those identified needs and resulting workforce planning, assess whether the acquisition workforce working capital fund as it currently operates is a sufficient mechanism to surge State's acquisition workforce capacity with the appropriate personnel, both in terms of expertise and numbers, and mix of government and contractor personnel to support State's missions in such environments and evaluate whether changes to the fund or other actions are needed.

2

3

Response: The Department concurs with this recommendation. We continue to hire additional USDH contracting staff; from 2008 until June 2012, State used its working capital fund (WCF) to hire an additional 66 staff, with 19 more in the pipeline. The Department of State's Office of Inspector General (OIG) conducted an entrance conference with A Bureau offices in July 2012, to specifically address the Department's application of the WCF to achieve key Procurement Shared Services goals, including workforce capacity. This just concluded GAO study and just initiated OIG study will be used to guide the Department's efforts to effectively support our acquisition needs.

3

Appendix III: GAO Contact and Staff Acknowledgments

GAO Contact	John P. Hutton, (202) 512-4841 or huttonj@gao.gov.
Acknowledgments	In addition to the contact named above, Johana R. Ayers, Assistant Director; Jessica Bull; Carole Coffey; Tara Copp; Thomas Costa; David Hancock; Meg Hardy; Kristine Hassinger; Melissa Hermes; Brandon L. Hunt; Hynek Kalkus; Gilbert Kim; Claire Li; Felicia M. Lopez; Judith A. McCloskey; Anne McDonough-Hughes; Lisa McMillen; Christopher Mulkins; Kenneth Patton; Jared Sippel; Roxanna T. Sun; Daniel Ramsey; Michael Rohrback; Anna Russell; Gwyneth B. Woolwine; and Matthew R. Young made key contributions to this report.

Related GAO Products

The following is a list of related products. For a full list of the most recent publications related to Iraq and Afghanistan, see http://www.gao.gov/docsearch/featured/oif.html.

Contingency Contracting: Agency Actions Needed to Address Recommendations by the Commission on Wartime Contracting in Iraq and Afghanistan. GAO-12-854R. Washington, D.C.: August 1, 2012.

Mission Iraq: State and DOD Face Challenges in Finalizing Support and Security Capabilities. GAO-12-856T. Washington, D.C.: June 28, 2012.

Operational Contract Support: Management and Oversight Improvements Needed in Afghanistan. GAO-12-290. Washington, D.C.: March 29, 2012.

Afghanistan: Improvements Needed to Strengthen Management of U.S. Civilian Presence. GAO-12-285. Washington, D.C.: February 27, 2012.

Iraq Drawdown: Opportunities Exist to Improve Equipment Visibility, Contractor Demobilization, and Clarity of Post-2011 DOD Role. GAO-11-774. Washington, D.C.: September 16, 2011.

Iraq and Afghanistan: DOD, State, and USAID Cannot Fully Account for Contracts, Assistance Instruments, and Associated Personnel. GAO-11-886. Washington, D.C.: September 15, 2011.

Contingency Contracting: Observations on Actions Needed to Address Systemic Challenges. GAO-11-580. Washington, D.C.: April 25, 2011.

Contingency Contracting: Improvements Needed in Management of Contractors Supporting Contract and Grant Administration in Iraq and Afghanistan. GAO-10-357. Washington, D.C.: April 12, 2010.

Warfighter Support: DOD Needs to Improve Its Planning for Using Contractors to Support Future Military Operation. GAO-10-472. Washington, D.C.: March 30, 2010.

Rebuilding Iraq: DOD and State Department Have Improved Oversight and Coordination of Private Security Contractors in Iraq, but Further Actions Are Needed to Sustain Improvements. GAO-08-966. Washington, D.C.: July 31, 2008.

Interagency Contracting: Need for Improved Information and Policy Implementation at the Department of State. GAO-08-578. Washington, D.C.: May 8, 2008.